Arthur DeMoss & David R. Enlow

HOW
TO CHANGE
YOUR WORLD
IN 12 WEEKS

SPIRE ♦ BOOKS

FLEMING H. REVELL COMPANY
OLD TAPPAN, NEW JERSEY

The Scripture quotations in this publication are taken from the *King James Version of the Bible,* unless otherwise identified.

The article "Five Minutes After" by Wayne Christianson is reprinted from *Moody Monthly* and is used by permission.

A Spire Book
ISBN 0-8007-8304-2
Published by
Fleming H. Revell Company
Old Tappan, New Jersey

How This Book Can Help You

LET'S GET RIGHT to the point: You can change your own private world—your life—in as short a span of time as three months; and it can be a drastic change. Gnawing doubts about your purpose in life, your accomplishments—even your degree of real, abiding happiness—qualify you for the life-changing adventure this volume offers.

To assist you in defining, pursuing and reaching certain goals in your life, the authors have asked distinguished business and professional men to share their actual experiences with you. As a part of this effort a two-day "Success Seminar" was held recently in Valley Forge, Pennsylvania, to help formulate the direction this book should take.

In addition to these leaders of business and industry, who were helpful from both literary and practical standpoints, some fifty other top executives and professional men from the United States and Canada collaborated with us on the general subject of success and the specific principles they considered vital in achieving worthwhile goals in life. Many of these men will be introduced in subsequent chapters. All have not necessarily "arrived"; they make no such claims for themselves, but along the way they have picked up some helpful pointers that they share willingly for our overall benefit. Like you, these men are still pursuing excellence, and they want it to be a balanced kind of excellence, as you do.

The *Success Diary,* at the end of each chapter, gives opportunity to score yourself on day-by-day accomplishments toward your goals and on specific traits or characteristics that will enable you to achieve them. This unique measurement also provides short questionnaires that test the effectiveness of your efforts to proceed toward an orderly goal.

If you are perfectly content with your life the way it is, this book is not for you. But, if you would like to have a new and improved outlook on life—an incentive for genuine success and a real purpose for living—you will want to read and heed every word.

Generally, this book deals with the subject of success. But how do you define success? It also deals with happiness. But how do you define happiness? We hope these preliminary pages will prove to be a helpful guide in motivating and preparing you for a thrilling twelve-week venture. Here is our definition of success: *making the maximum use of one's God-given abilities in the pursuit and progressive attainment of a specific goal in harmony with God's will.* But even that specific goal can change from time to time, which necessitates day-by-day alertness to the direction of your life.

We must be careful not to dogmatize in relation to success and goals. For example, one person—you, perhaps—may be striving toward a lifelong goal, which has been made abundantly clear to you as God's will for your life. Another person may be clearly led in a "secular" field for a time, then his goals may be clearly reoriented toward more specific spiritual service for a subsequent period of time. Or two secular or two spiritual goals might be involved. Is one more "right" than another? Surely not, for examples abound on every hand to duplicate such experiences.

Ideally, there should never be any delineation between the sacred and the secular insofar as the Christian is concerned. The person who lays bricks or teaches children or performs the normal duties of a housewife can be so obviously in the center of God's will for his life that even the humblest task becomes sacred. Figuratively, turning on a bright light, or even a dim one, in a place of utter darkness is a spiritual act in every sense of the word, although many times it is performed unconsciously.

The Bible's "successful" men—Moses, David, Paul and many others—were all men who failed in one way or another. And yet, the God who looks upon the heart found in each of these men a will bent upon acceding to His way and His will in every area of life.

A top pediatrician in the East faced this question in his life: Should he seek to excel in his field, to become one of the leading specialists in the world? If so, he would have to give up several forms of Christian and community service in which he had been engaged. Because he chose to maintain a balanced program of religious activity and professional endeavor is he any less a success? Hardly.

If the Westminster Catechism is correct in its assessment of goals—"Man's chief end is to glorify God and to enjoy Him forever"—then, of course, it throws a whole new light on the subject. Analyzed carefully, that statement sums up what should be supremely worthy of attainment. God is the only person worthy of glory; to enjoy something necessarily implies that the subject

5

is experiencing joy, which surely must include happiness in its most essential forms.

But all of this must be broken down into various areas of your life: (1) business or professional (housewife, student, lawyer, etc.); (2) home; (3) social; (4) church. In each of the twelve principles discussed, therefore—one for each week—we seek to consider all four areas of life, insofar as that particular characteristic or trait is concerned.

Some authorities believe that if success is not your primary goal in life, you may be seeking happiness. Still others assert that the thing most sought after in life by many people is to be a worthwhile member of a worthwhile group. We try to touch base on each of these points, so that whichever you prefer you can feel a solid measure of achievement.

Of necessity, the authors, in counsel with their many assistants, had to come to some agreement as to what comprises an ideal—something toward which we are all striving. If you complete the *Success Diary* at the end of each chapter—alone or in company with someone in whom you regularly confide—you will be helped toward reaching this ideal. You can be helped even if you do *not* complete the *Success Diary,* but the experience certainly should prove beneficial—and exciting— if you face up to the questions and grading that make up the *Success Diary.*

We proceed on the assumption that you, like the authors, have not yet reached this ideal. Therefore, we are all on common territory. But many have enjoyed experiences that can help the rest of us along the way, unlocking doors that have kept hidden some invaluable secrets. One unlocked secret, quickened to your personal need, can be worth many times the cost of this volume. Some thrilling discovery may revolutionize your life, even as it has for the authors.

As our co-laborers have reminded us, down through the ages, even the greatest of men have had their weaknesses. A man who is completely successful in his business or profession may turn out to be a total failure in his family relations. Similarly a person may become an ideal husband and father, or wife and mother, yet not quite make the grade in other areas of his or her life. One aim of this book is to strive toward well-rounded, balanced living.

At least one important assumption is made by the authors: Believers in the Lord Jesus Christ, who thus possess God's Holy Spirit as an indwelling force in their lives, are possessing or striving consciously towards the fruit of the Spirit—love, joy, peace, long-suffering, gentleness, goodness, meekness, faith, temperance (self-control). This assumption eliminates the necessity for a sermon on the subject of the fruit of the Holy Spirit and enables us to proceed with what some might term less "spiritual" qualities that lead to success and happiness.

No attempt has been made to be all-comprehensive in suggesting traits of character that are desirable and necessary. Only a dozen major ones are mentioned, but cultivation of these can alter drastically the course of your life.

Contents

Where Are You Going?

Ask yourself one important question before you proceed further: What is my principal talent—the one thing on which I can concentrate? Like the Apostle Paul you can then say, "This one thing I do," instead of "These fifty things I dabble in."

Many Christians, content to sit on the sidelines as spectators in the great spiritual warfare called life, have never really entered the fray by setting meaningful and worthwhile goals. In the words of G. Tom Willey, recently retired Martin Company executive: "People do not plan to fail; they fail to plan." If this is true in your life, you can be helped immeasurably by the counsel, example and gentle persuasion of others who are traveling the same pathway.

Napoleon Hill, whose book *Think and Grow Rich* has been read by perhaps seven million men and women, lists twelve great riches of life: a positive mental attitude, sound physical health, harmony in human relationships, freedom from all forms of fear, the hope of future achievement, the capacity for faith, willingness to share one's blessings, a labor of love as an occupation, an open mind on all subjects, self-discipline in all circumstances, the capacity to understand others, sufficient money.

Certainly one measure of success in your life concerns the priorities you have established. Are they material, physical, spiritual—or a combination of all three? Ideally, they should embrace the four major areas of life previously referred to: business or professional, home, social, church.

The Oriental idea of success seems to be entirely different from that of most areas of the world. When Mrs. George Romney, wife of the governor of Michigan, visited the Far East, the question she encountered most frequently was "How are your American children turning out?" That is a vital question and one that influences any meaningful measure of success.

Sociologists point out the "alternation of generations," whereby one generation of young people may be quiet and passive, only to be followed by an extremely activist group such as we have today. Certainly environment plays a part in the overall picture, for young people—their elders, too—often are like sheep in their determination to follow the crowd.

The salutatorian of a recent high-school graduating class was assigned this topic for her brief address: "The Protesting Generation: on the National Level." Perhaps this subject is typical of many commencement and baccalaureate messages in the present era, for we do live in an age of rebellion. But our young people today have many justifiable grounds for protest.

Rebellion against authority, all too often, stems from adults. Witness the protests of all kinds, the demonstrations, the riots, that more often than not have their stimuli in the "leadership" of an older person who should know better. To some, breaking the law is a mark of distinction and is considered justified by the merit of the particular case.

The overwhelming majority of young people today, however, do not fall into the category of extremist, despite the blaring headlines and the chaotic scenes on television. Someone wisely suggested that a moratorium on press, radio and television coverage of today's strikes, riots and demonstrations—especially on TV—might bring about an amazing easing of tension in many areas of our public life. The thought is worthy of serious consideration.

What we are trying to say is simply this: If you want to change your world—in twelve *weeks* or twelve *months*—the process must begin with *you*, not with a mass demonstration that more often than not merely confuses the issue. The answer to the world's problems —nationally, internationally, politically and spiritually—lies not in legislation or reform but in a better *you*, and a better *me*. Your own private world and the great global world in which you live will show a marked change for the better as you determine to reorient the course of your life right here and now.

What motivation controls your life? This is vitally important. Why do you do the things you do and say the things you say? Have you ever thought seriously about the subject? Someone once pointed out that although the spiritual side of life is, by and large, intangible in terms of measurement, it deserves primary attention.

God, our Creator, loves each one of us—*you* included—and He has a perfect blueprint for our lives. The pursuit of this plan, by enabling us to make maximum use of all our talents and abilities, provides us with the purpose and direction which we each sorely need in this life. And the attainment of this plan—made practical and possible in these pages—provides the greatest satisfaction and happiness in this life, and it is real and lasting.

But God will not force His will and plan on anyone. We must deliberately seek out His blueprint for our lives. To accomplish this, at least three things must be considered: (1) we must stop and take inventory of our lives; (2) we must determine to want only the perfect, directive (rather than merely permissive) will of God for our lives, regardless of cost or consequences; (3) we must be flexible, open-minded; check out every possibility—every open door—without preconceived notions or predetermined conclusions, praying constantly for God's perfect plan.

Upon determining God's will for your life, you will want to set a specific goal in harmony with it. Day-by-day, even moment-by-moment, helps toward this end are provided in these pages. The very first chapter, in fact, will launch you on a twelve-week adventure that can change your life dramatically.

Commenting on the necessity for goals, Charles Dunne, president of Dunne's Insurance Reports, said: "The man who has no objective other than to live from day to day and on a hand-to-mouth basis has too many temptations." It is strange, indeed, that even believers in Christ often are content to go along with little or no sense of mission. Small wonder, then, that so many experience confusion, disillusionment and even despair, for they have not taken the time to discover for themselves just where they are headed and why.

"The man who has a destination in mind," declared Robert Thornton, Jr., president of Mercantile National Bank, Dallas, Texas, "may sometimes have to get off the main highway and take a detour. He may have to back up or circle around, but because he knows where he wants to go he eventually gets there. The man with no destination in mind never gets back on the main highway once he takes a detour."

Down through the years successful men and women, without exception, have been those who had clearly fixed goals and burning desire. Napoleon Hill outlined six ways to turn desires into success. One of his ardent admirers and followers was Thomas A. Edison, who placed his stamp of approval upon the six ways by declaring them not only essential for the accumulation of money, but for the attainment of any goal. Slightly paraphrasing Hill's six ways, by substituting goals for money, we arrive at these rules:

1) Fix in your mind the specific goal you desire. It is not sufficient merely to say, "I want to reach some general goal." Be definite as to the particular goal.

2) Determine exactly what you intend to give in return for the goal you desire. (Remember, there is no such reality as "something for nothing.")

3) Establish a definite date to reach the goal you desire.

4) Create a definite plan for carrying out your desire and begin at once, whether you are ready or not, to put this plan into action.

5) Write out a clear, concise statement of the goal you intend to reach. Name the time limit for its attainment, state what you intend to give in exchange, and describe clearly the plan through which you intend to accomplish it.

6) Read your written statement aloud, twice daily, once just before retiring at night and once after arising in the morning. As you read, *see* and *feel* and *believe* that you already have attained the goal.

Lest this seem like little more than a vigorous exercise in positive thinking, we should remind you from the Bible that "as [a man] thinketh in his heart, so is he." Thought precedes action, and practical steps are necessary before any degree of success is achieved.

"There is a price men must pay to achieve success and the price is never cheap," declared Lee S. Bickmore, Chairman of the Board of the National Biscuit Company, in a recent address before the Illinois State Chamber of Commerce. "There are no bargains at the leadership counter. But the effort to achieve it represents the finest genius given to man."

Bickmore cited four price tags on success: painstaking preparations; helping others to grow; high aim; long days and sleepless nights. "If you don't want to pay this price, you had better not shop at the leadership counter," he added. "Today we have agitation for shorter work weeks; we see individuals encouraged to assume less responsibility for their own actions and to seek security. Yet no man ever became a great leader or a great success on an eight-hour day."

Such truths are clearly delineated in this volume, and it is shown that the principles whereby men and women achieve success and true happiness, in the real sense of the words, are age-old principles which have their basis in the Bible. We demonstrate that these principles can be appropriated and utilized by each of us, regardless of our social, educational, cultural, economic or religious background. As you read these pages we would encourage you to:

Underscore pertinent definitions, illustrations, ideas and principles. Memorize appropriate verses from the Bible, definitions of principles involved and steps for achieving each principle. Review each chapter carefully during the week, as you seek to score yourself in the *Success Diary*. You will be surprised, if not amazed, at the results. Apply the principles specifically and rigidly to your own life, until they have become a part of you.

You *can* be a success—in your own eyes as well as in those of others. Prove it as you read these pages. Before you begin to read Chapter 1 and its first exciting step toward a new you, take a few moments to set one primary goal in your life, along with any secondary goals that seem to be uppermost in your mind. The exercise will do you good!

MY PRIMARY GOAL ————————————————

————————————————————————————

SECONDARY GOALS (*if any*) ——————————————

————————————————————————————

1.

How Open-minded Am I?

ONE ABSOLUTE essential to success in life is *receptivity,* which includes *1*) the ability to accept criticism, rebuke, taunts, gracefully; *2*) the gift of enlarging one's capacity. All of the principles referred to in these pages hinge on this one attribute, for without it one has no assurance he will be open to the other eleven. Too often our ability to take it depends upon the state of our health, or our emotional outlook at the particular time, or some other consideration. But the fact remains that the truly successful person cultivates an attitude toward life and toward people that is not contingent upon whim and circumstance.

Beginning at the crack of dawn, when the first tentative step is taken away from the comforts of bed, the person who is truly going somewhere is the one who acts rather than reacts, even—and especially— among members of his own family. The grouchy or complaining tone of a wife, husband, or child, for example, may not set the pattern for the day; but it presents an opportunity for receptivity, the ability to learn from complaints, criticism or a negative attitude.

That first encounter with the outside world—at the office, in the classroom, or in the home—will loom primarily as another opportunity to learn to respond with a positive attitude and an open heart and mind. Truly, all of life becomes a rich adventure when it is approached with genuine receptivity. The minutes and hours are all too short; the day rushes by. Almost every second is cherished as an invaluable gift that must be well-spent rather than wasted.

A proper frame of mind is vitally important as one opens his heart to receive truth. Famed orchestra leader Meredith Willson described an unusual experience of his in humorous but perceptive imagery. As a young man from Boone, Iowa, Willson had made good in the music world. He went to New York for further studies, determined to grasp every opportunity to make maximum use of his God-given talents.

One night he had a dream, in which a great king spoke to all of the members of the orchestra in which Willson played the piccolo. "If you will each bring your instrument to me," the monarch said, "I will fill it with pure gold." The men reacted gleefully—here indeed was an offer they could ill afford to miss. Meredith Willson watched his fellow musicians parade toward the king. First came the drummer, eager and ready. Though hampered somewhat by the size of his instrument he wasted no time in responding. Quickly his big bass drum was filled with gold. He marched triumphantly away, joyful at the prompt fulfillment of the promise.

Then came the player of the bass fiddle, his eager eyes already grasping the coveted prize. The king, true to his promise, faithfully stuffed the instrument with the precious metal, right to the brim, and the happy fiddler strode away. One by one each musician received his gift and left rejoicing, each in turn content with his portion of the prize. But poor Meredith Willson—*there he stood with his piccolo!*

In similar fashion many people today sit at the banquet table of potential success—piled high with gourmet delights—and they come away with only crumbs. They have been blind to the table spread before them, or unbelieving that it was really theirs, or strangely fearful of partaking for imagined reasons. As the Bible says, they receive not because they ask not. Receptivity implies positive action as well as passive acceptance—*action* rather than *reaction*. It is not enough to stand idly by and expect to reap a harvest.

Like Meredith Willson, you can stand with your piccolo and receive minimal blessing or you can bring your English horn of humility and openness and open the way for every kind of help imaginable. But the matter of receptivity is a personal one: you alone can exercise your will in this regard. To achieve success in the world, regardless of one's definition of the word, one must come with open mind and hand and heart to receive all of the good that man and Creator would make available to him. Closed minds and closed hearts rule out the very touchstone of success.

Former Governor Frank Clement of Tennessee, one of more than fifty outstanding Americans who contributed their views to this volume, told the authors: "If you will read your Bible you will find that nearly every significant truth it contains was revealed in the course of a personal encounter between human beings. Whether it was the wise men coming to Bethlehem or Mary Magdalene bringing her alabaster vase to the Master, everybody who comes to see you brings precious gifts. The wisdom to find and to profit from the treasure that daily comes through your office door is one of the inescapable hallmarks of success." The former governor, known for his "open door policy" to visitors at the Executive Mansion in Nashville, quoted Calvin Coolidge as saying, "Nobody ever listened himself out of a job."

Many traits, habits, characteristics, principles—call them what you will—have marked the world's successful people down through the ages. Conscious, deliberate determination to cultivate these qualities is an essential part of one's growth, if one is to find success in the fullest sense of the word. That is why it is imperative for you to make this effort in a practical, regular way, which accounts for the *Success Diary,* the vitally important, climaxing segment of each chapter.

We encourage you to maintain this diary in the suggested fashion faithfully and conscientiously, first by answering the questions each day for a week. We can guarantee you, from personal experience, that Scriptural principles leading to unqualified success will be made to live in a new way, as you see them being fulfilled in your very own life. For the sake of clarity read and heed carefully these suggestions:

1) After you have completed the reading of this chapter on *receptivity,* begin the very next day—for a period of exactly one full week—to keep the accompanying daily record of your adherence to this particular trait.

2) Every morning, without fail, review the chapter's closing suggestions on "How To Be Receptive." Throughout the day, by deliberate concentration, determine to be receptive to every voice that seeks to help you, even though the help may be in the guise of criticism, rebuke or taunt.

3) For a full week make this one thought of receptivity uppermost in your mind and heart. It will make you alert to every golden door of opportunity for learning, for service, for success.

4) Be completely honest in scoring yourself on this particular trait. No one else need see the results, but *you* will know the areas that need building up and cultivating.

After a week of concentration on the subject of *receptivity,* you should be in a position to focus your attention on the subject of the next chapter, which is *enthusiasm.* That chapter, of course, is one you should be reading during the week of practical attention to the subject of receptivity, so you may move progressively forward toward achievment of all the traits that culminate in genuine success.

If you are the type of reader who usually plows manfully through an entire book at one sitting, we urge you to change your ways in this instance. But, if you must read it all the way through from force of habit, after you have read it, start again at the beginning with Chapter 1—taking a chapter at a time —and proceed as suggested. We ask that you score yourself a week at a time on the particular principle outlined for the seven-day period. You will note that the previous week's major goal is carried forward the following week as a minor goal, which should help you form a solid chain of attainment as you score yourself on two different principles for each week after the first one. Specific instructions within each chapter should make all of this crystal clear as you proceed.

Positive thinking *alone* can never accomplish what this book sets out to do; such thinking must be fol-

lowed by positive action on your part. With certain
guidelines contained herein this should pose no problem. Why not be the success that you want to be and
that your Creator intended you should be?

How To Be Receptive

1. Accept criticism, rebuke, taunts gracefully; actively
   seek helps, ideas, constructive criticism.
2. Be a good listener.
3. Deliberately determine to acquiesce to the still
   small voice of God as He speaks to you through
   the Holy Spirit.
4. When you read the Bible (four pages a day to finish
   in a year) proceed with this attitude: "Open thou
   mine eyes, that I may behold wondrous things out
   of thy law" (Psalm 119:18).

How Open-minded Am I?

Answer *yes* or *no*. Statements that are not applicable
to your life on a specific day should not be counted in
your score for that day. Eight or more *yes* answers
superior; six or seven, *excellent;* four or five, *good;*
two or three, *fair;* one or none, *poor.*

1. When a suggestion came to me from a member of
   my family, this morning, I took it without resentment.
2. When the boss (or teacher, or other superior) gave
   me his first directive of the day, my reaction was
   good.
3. When my employee passed along his idea to me, or
   registered a complaint, I took it well.

4. In reading the newspaper, at least one valuable item of information impressed itself upon me.

5. That helpful hint via radio or television has registered itself strongly upon my mind.

6. When my mind has reverted to some apparent slight of the past, I have been able to put the best possible interpretation upon it.

7. I have not given a cold shoulder to anyone who came to me with counsel or with question.

8. My Bible or devotional reading this morning taught me at least one helpful lesson.

9. Something my Sunday-school teacher or pastor said last Sunday has stood me in good stead today.

10. My approach to spiritual truths has been: "Open thou mine eyes, that I may behold wondrous things out of thy law" (Psalm 119:18).

SUCCESS DIARY

Week No. 1   **Dates**......................19...... to ....19......

Major Goal: Be Receptive!

(Check appropriate score for each day)

Achievement of Goal	Superior	Excellent	Good	Fair	Poor
Sunday					
Monday					
Tuesday					
Wednesday					
Thursday					
Friday					
Saturday					

Remarks:

2.
Do I Have That Extra Spark?

RARELY in the history of man has a person ever become an outstanding success, by any definition of the word, without *enthusiasm*. The hundreds of popular self-help books now on the market attest to this fact. But many an individual today has long since given up the idea of being enthusiastic about the prosaic, unexciting work to which he has been called. If you fall into this category, an awakening is in order, and quickly!

The Scriptural basis for enthusiasm is written in the form of a command: "And whatsoever ye do, do it heartily, as to the Lord, and not unto men" (Colossians 3:23). And no command is recorded in Holy Writ that is impossible of fulfillment. Some incidents in our lives—promotions, recognitions, achievements of loved ones, awards, vacations, weddings—do not require any particular effort to work up enthusiasm. It comes with the package. But when effort is required, it can be eminently worthwhile on a number of counts.

At times, even the most satisfactory and enjoyable of jobs can become routine and drab. When that happens, exercise your mind in accord with the principle, ". . . as [a man thinketh] in his heart, so is he" (Proverbs 23:7). As you walk or drive or ride to work in the morning or, as you begin the day's housekeeping or start another day in school, force yourself to become enthusiastic about the tasks ahead of you. Determine deliberately in your mind and heart that the day's duties will not only deserve and receive your very best, but that you will approach them enthusiastically. A surprising thing will take place, as it has with the authors on many occasions: if you *act* enthusiastic, very shortly you will find yourself *becoming* and *being* enthusiastic.

When the Bible speaks of obedience being better than sacrifice it is establishing a divine principle that is true in every area of life. *Obey,* then receive the promise. The Scriptural injunction is: ". . . whatsoever ye do, do it heartily, as to the Lord . . ." and obedience to that command will always bring the desired result—in this particular instance, enthusiasm. Many top leaders in the business and professional world echo the necessity for this particular trait.

A few weeks before his death in October of 1966, at the age of ninety-nine, five-and-ten-cent store pioneer S. S. Kresge told the authors: "One of the most important ingredients in a person's makeup for successful business operations is enthusiasm. This extra spark is often the deciding factor in selling a good idea, making a worthwhile sale or developing and maintaining a successful and loyal organization." That kind of enthusiasm has no limit to its potentialities.

When a young North Carolina minister, in his unbounded enthusiasm for his calling, preached to the stately palm trees near Tampa, Florida, a few years ago, he did more than set the stage for an unprecedented evangelistic ministry around the world—second to none in history. Billy Graham's enthusiasm has influenced many other lives and has molded the character of many young people. One of these was Louis Christensen, now an executive in Orlando, Florida.

For eight years Christensen served as state young people's president for his denomination. One of his vice presidents was the lanky young North Carolinian who was then studying in Florida. "Billy's enthusiasm as a young pastor," Christensen says, "had a marked effect on my life." Today, in Christensen's business responsibilities and in his duties as a Director of Christian Business Men's Committee International, he reflects marked enthusiasm in all of his undertakings.

The effect of a sincere display of good, old-fashioned enthusiasm—the kind that is not afraid to vent itself in behalf of a desired goal or end—is incalculable. Noted news commentator Paul Harvey has strong views on the subject: "If I could shake the shoulders of every youngster today, and could command his concentration on one thing I have to say. . . . If I could have five minutes with every student, with every young man or woman his first day on a new job. . . . If I could burn one message into the consciousness of all whose minds are not yet closed, whose consciences are not yet calloused with cynicism, this is it: *Nowadays you can do such big things with such lit le effort*. Such a little diligence, such a little discipline, such a little pleasantness, such a little determination, such a little *enthusiasm* . . . is all it takes to distinguish an uncommon man, an exceptional woman."

Paul Harvey is not alone in his views. J. Elliott Stedelbauer, recent chairman of Christian Business Men's Committee International and president of El-Sted Investments, Inc., Toronto, Ontario, told the authors: "To be a good salesman, a person has to have what I like to call organized enthusiasm. He must know his product and his prospects. He must realize that the key to success is hard work, enthusiasm and effectiveness. Not very many worthwhile things in life come to the average person without the persistent application of these basic principles."

Other top executives express similar views. The president of one of the nation's largest transit corporations was asked what he considered the greatest single spur to success, by Paul J. Meyer, dynamic young founder of Success Motivation Institute, Inc., Waco, Texas. The president replied: "The longer I live the more certain I am that enthusiasm is the little recognized secret of success. The difference in actual skill, ability and intelligence between those who succeed and those who fail is usually neither wide nor striking. But if two men are equally matched, the man who is enthusiastic will find the scales tipped in his favor."

Meyer added that "a man of second-rate ability with enthusiasm will generally outstrip the one of first-rate ability without enthusiasm. Believe in your work . . . love it . . . whether it's digging a ditch or directing a corporation. To an enthusiastic man, work is always part play . . . regardless of how hard or demanding it may be. A man in this frame of mind is powered with dynamite; he's headed for the stars. True enthusiasm is a combination of two human factors: intellect and emotion. It springs from the heart and is as difficult to hide as is great sorrow or abiding love. The power of enthusiasm lies in its natural and unrestrained expression."

One can understand this evaluation of the trait much better when he learns the root meaning of the word.

Miss Michael Drury, writing in *Glamour* Magazine, pointed out that "the word enthusiasm comes from *entheos*—the god within—and means basically to be inspired or possessed by the god, or, if you like, by God. It is the open secret, as commonplace and tireless as sunlight, that gives joy and purpose to all our days, if only we don't despise it. The taproot of enthusiasm is learning."

Not only learning but also determination and *esprit de corps* play vital parts in the cultivation of enthusiasm. Many an athletic contest has been won by the weaker team because the enthusiastic support of fans has generated a keener enthusiasm on the part of the athletes themselves. This same principle is true in many areas of life. The enthusiastic teacher, engrossed in and excited about his subject, unconsciously transmits that same spirit of adventure to his students, and they respond with growing interest to the delightful discoveries of the subject. The employer in the business world who approaches his work with eager delight is quite likely to have a staff of enthusiastic employees. And that employee who shows zest in his duties wins the attention of his superiors and rightfully earns for himself any available promotions.

A sage once observed that although many men are born to be giants, few grow above common men, because they lack enthusiasm. Something magnetic attaches itself to one with this particular characteristic. Most people like to be around the individual who has a zest for living. One cannot long remain near an outgoing enthusiast without following one of two courses: joining in or making a hasty exit. It is hard to remain neutral in the presence of an exuberant person.

Some may think the value of this principle is overestimated. But not Sir Edward Victor Appleton. When he had been knighted by the King of England, awarded the Nobel Prize in Physics and made Chancellor of the University of Edinburgh, *Time* Magazine wired him to ask if he had any recipe for success. "Yes," he replied, "enthusiasm. I rate that even ahead of professional skill."

Displays of sincere enthusiasm inevitably lead to surprising results. U.S. Government official L. Sterling Hedgpeth, now on duty in Ecuador, has been building highways and airports for the Bureau of Public Roads, the Army Engineers and various foreign aid administrations (MSA, FOA, ICA, and AID). He has worked for Uncle Sam on six continents.

Not until Hedgpeth reached his present locale of Quito, Ecuador, did he encounter a display of enthusiasm that transformed his life. A university chum gave him the names of two men in Ecuador: a staff member of Radio Station HCJB in Quito and a pilot of the Missionary Aviation Fellowship. Hedgpeth visited the home of the radio official first. There he met a family who rejoiced at having given up a lucrative vice-presidency in a United States firm, having sold home, car and yacht and having come to Ecuador to share their faith. Hedgpeth wrote them off as the usual missionary fanatics. "However," he confessed, "I knew deep down inside that these people had something I needed and wanted. All the memories of self-condemnation, unhappiness and lack of mental peace of the past years flooded over me."

Friends invited Hedgpeth to two Sunday evening programs broadcast by HCJB. He encountered unbounded enthusiasm on the part of some one hundred staff members, and their professional ability as musicians impressed him deeply. "The complete and thorough dedication of their lives, the sense of urgency of everyone connected with the station, and primarily their enthusiasm won me over," he said.

Even though he probably never heard of Sterling Hedgpeth, automobile tycoon Walter Chrysler summed up the situation well: "The real secret of success is enthusiasm. Yes, more than enthusiasm I would say excitement. I like to see men get excited. When they get excited they make a success of their lives." Your own life can be changed dramatically by faithful employment of enthusiasm that leads to excitement. It is never too early in life, nor too late, to begin.

How To Be Enthusiastic

1. Obey the Scriptural command, "Whatsoever ye do, do it heartily, as to the Lord."
2. If you don't feel enthusiastic, *act* enthusiastic; soon you will *feel* enthusiastic and *be* enthusiastic.
3. Let yourself go as you would at an athletic contest or a political rally or a family reunion.

Do I Have That Extra Spark?

Answer *yes* or *no*. Statements that are not applicable to your life on a specific day should not be counted in your score for that day. Eight or more *yes* answers: *superior;* six or seven, *excellent;* four or five, *good;* two or three, *fair;* one or none, *poor.*

1. Even before my first cup of coffee (tea, or milk) I was able to feel some degree of enthusiasm about my plans for the day.

2. Lacking any slight feeling of enthusiasm when I awoke, I dwelt on encouraging, optimistic thoughts until my outlook changed for the better.

3. I have deliberately cultivated an exuberant mood by proceeding wholeheartedly into my endeavors for the day.

4. My attitudes and actions have paved the way for genuine enthusiasm by enabling me to have an easy conscience.

5. Today, I have consciously kept the thought of enthusiasm uppermost in my mind.

6. I have been aware of the fact that my display of enthusiasm has affected someone else favorably.

7. My children (parents, wife, husband) have known that my present work—as businessman, professional man, housewife or student—has had my complete attention today.

8. I have been able to overcome mental and physical hindrances on the way to displaying enthusiasm.

9. Even at the end of a grueling day on the job (in the office, at home, at school) I find a reservoir of genuine enthusiasm within me.

10. My devotional reading for the day has served to improve my enthusiastic outlook.

SUCCESS DIARY

Week No. 2   Dates.....................19...... to ....19......

Major Goal: Be Enthusiastic!
Minor Goal: Be Receptive!

(Check appropriate scores for each day)

Achievement of Goals		Superior	Excellent	Good	Fair	Poor
Sunday	(Major)					
	(Minor)					
Monday	(Major)					
	(Minor)					
Tuesday	(Major)					
	(Minor)					
Wednesday	(Major)					
	(Minor)					
Thursday	(Major)					
	(Minor)					
Friday	(Major)					
	(Minor)					
Saturday	(Major)					
	(Minor)					

Remarks:

3.
Am I on the Right Track?

ONE OF THE foremost champions of the quality of
single-mindedness was the great steel magnate and
philanthropist, Andrew Carnegie, who once told an
audience of college students: "Here is the prime condition of success, the great secret. Concentrate your
energy, thought and capital exclusively upon the business in which you are engaged. Having begun in one
line, resolve to fight it out on that line, to lead in it;
adopt every improvement, have the best machinery and
know the most about it."

Carnegie added: "The concerns which fail are those
which have scattered their capital, which means that
they have scattered their brains also. They have investments in this, or that, or the other, here, there and
everywhere. 'Don't put all your eggs in one basket'
is all wrong. I tell you, *'Put all your eggs in one basket,
and then watch that basket, day and night.'* Look
around you and take notice. Men who do that do not
often fail. It is easy to watch and carry the one basket.
It is trying to carry too many baskets that breaks most
eggs in this country. He who carries three baskets
must put one on his head, which is apt to tumble and
trip him up. One fault of the American businessman is
lack of concentration."

This principle of single-mindedness has many noted adherents. One who feels strongly on the subject is famed CBS commentator Walter Cronkite. "I'm convinced that the real secret of success is to keep your eye on the road immediately ahead," he says.

The same characteristic is needed by the housewife, the student, the pastor. While it is true that our work in the home, at the office or shop and in the church may involve a variety of duties, it is equally true that all of them *can* and *should* be done with an eye single to the glory of God. This is single-mindedness of the highest order.

Phrasing it another way, Ralph Waldo Emerson—philosopher, poet, essayist and lecturer—declared: "The world will always make room for the man who knows where he's going."

One such man is Dr. William Bright, founder of the burgeoning Campus Crusade for Christ organization, whose burden for the spiritual welfare of students so engrossed him that his one-man operation of ten years ago has grown to worldwide proportions, commanding the best talents of more than twelve hundred full-time workers and countless thousands of others who now share his vision. Though he respects, honors and co-operates with all organizations and individuals engaged in the task of fulfilling the Great Commission, Bright has an eye single to the work to which he feels called.

This dedication to a task is also a prime essential for the military man who would accomplish his purpose in life. Lieutenant General William K. Harrison (U. S. Army, Retired), who distinguished himself at the Panmunjom peace table terminating the Korean conflict, told the authors: "Success is the achievement of a goal which one sets for himself. If one's ultimate goal is kept in mind and pursued with determination, using such abilities, initiative, imagination and wisdom as may be possessed, he may finally reach it. My own military career may be used as an example.

"I never had any desire to be wealthy, only to be a soldier, and this naturally meant that high command was the goal chosen. This stimulated me to hard work and professional study, and the determinaton to do each assignment well. I have no doubt that everyone who reaches high military rank has followed more or less the same course. The true goal of man must be to please the Creator, who necessarily possesses the right to his life and all that he has. Of course, if one simply chooses to be a rebel, that he can be, and take the unhappy consequences. I give thanks to God for whatever success I may have had in the military profession, because I know that whatever talents I may have had were His gifts and He guided my career in accord with His purpose for my life."

The simplicity of such an uncluttered life is beautiful to behold. And, although it is uncommon, this quality of life can be found in a number of places and is worth working toward. Texas industrialist-inventor R. G. LeTourneau illustrates the point well: "You've heard of the dog that chased a freight train and when he caught it didn't know what to do with it. I guess he had a dog's day while he was on the run, but all his effort ended in disappointment. It would have been a tale with a different ending if he had gone after a cat or a rabbit, but he spent his precious energy chasing an iron horse that couldn't reward him with a single juicy bone."

LeTourneau continues: "It is a good thing to take

stock of life now and again to ask, 'What am I chasing? What are the objectives of my life?' I can't help wondering whether that dog took a good look before he streaked off after that train. Maybe his hound nature made him chase it just because it moved. He didn't stop to ask whether the effort was worthwhile. Too many lives are being spent in the pursuit of unworthy things, which will issue at last in bitter disillusionment. Only as we 'set our affection on things above' can we be sure of avoiding disappointment. To reach the borders of eternity and then to realize that we have been chasing freight trains and ignoring the priceless blessings offered in Jesus Christ will be the greatest tragedy of all.''

Even while one performs a variety of duties or engages in several different activities simultaneously, one need not ''chase freight trains.'' Take the case of the former captain of the Harvard basketball team —Eugene B. Augustine, Jr., of Binghamton, New York. It could hardly be said that his eye was single to the success of the team's basketball fortunes, even though he always played to win and gave the best of himself in every game, for at the age of twelve he had made a life commitment that affected his every endeavor thereafter.

''I have always loved competition,'' Augustine said, ''particularly in athletics. Regardless of the sport the ever-present challenge to win and excel has always fascinated me and inevitably driven me to diligent practice. The thrill of competing and winning has always elated me, but a far greater source of satisfaction to me has been the new life which I received the day that I received Jesus Christ as Lord and Saviour. The joy of living for a purpose, namely to honor

Christ through every endeavor, has surpassed any athletic triumph I have experienced. The ever-present reality of a new spiritual dimension has filled the vacuum which my soul felt.''

Another athlete, even more renowned than the Ivy League basketball star, pointed to a man with a single purpose in life as one who had made an indelible impact upon him. Babe Ruth, one of the all-time great home-run hitters and a member of the New York Yankees, said: ''Most of the people who have really counted in my life were not famous. Nobody ever heard of them, except those who knew and loved them. I knew an old minister once. His hair was white, his face shone. I have written my name on thousands and thousands of baseballs in my life. The old minister wrote his name on just a few simple hearts. How I envy him! He was not trying to please his own immortal soul. So fame never came to him. I am listed as a famous home-runner; yet beside that obscure minister who was so good and so wise I never got to first base.''

Babe Ruth's friend had learned a wonderful lesson. That person who is intent on being a servant, first to his Creator and then to his fellowman—who has an eye single to the glory of God—will make several important discoveries along life's pathway. For one thing, his own heart and mind will be at peace—a condition that is prized and highly sought after by millions of people today. Then, too, he will have the inner assurance that his life counts for something, which provides a satisfaction that money cannot buy.

No person should continue through life without an overriding purpose leading him on, one that is worthy of a man's greatest efforts—blood, sweat and tears, if need be. Remember, "a double-minded man is unstable in all his ways." Add stability to your life by concentrating on a single goal.

Such stability has characterized the successful person in all ages. In a study of more than five hundred of the world's great leaders, success author Napoleon Hill learned the secret of their successes and found a single trait common to all: *Every man, without exception, had a specific goal toward which he set himself.* He moved toward that goal with tremendous zeal. He allowed nothing to stand in his way. This may seem ruthless, but it is a necessity to the person who wants to succeed in life.

Too often, this type of single-mindedness is exemplified by those who are supporting an empty hope. A young Communist, in a letter to one of his friends back home, typifies this spirit:

What seems of first importance to you is to me either not desirable or impossible of realization. But there is one thing about which I am in dead earnest—and that is the socialist cause. It is my life, business, my religion, my hobby, my sweetheart, wife and mistress, my bread and meat. I work at it in the daytime and dream of it at night. Its hold on me grows, not lessens, as time goes on. I'll be in it the rest of my life. It is my alter ego. When you think of me, it is necessary to think of socialism as well, because I'm inseparably bound to it.

Therefore I can't carry on a friendship, a love affair, or even a conversation without relating it to this force which both drives and guides my life. I evaluate people, books, ideas and notions according to how they affect the socialist cause and by their attitude toward it. I have already been in jail because of my ideas, and if necessary I am ready to go before a firing squad. A certain percentage of us get killed or imprisoned. Even for those who escape these harsher ends, life is no bed of roses. A genuine radical lives in virtual poverty. He turns back to the party every penny he makes above what is absolutely necessary to keep him alive.

We constantly look for places where the class struggle is the sharpest, exploiting these situations to the limit of their possibilities. We lead strikes. We organize demonstrations. We speak on street corners. We fight cops. We go through trying experiences many times each year which the ordinary man has to face only once or twice in a lifetime. And when we're not doing these more exciting things, all our spare time is taken up with dull routine chores, endless leg work, errands, etc., which are inescapably connected with running a live organization.

Radicals don't have the time or the money for many movies or concerts or T-bone steaks or decent homes and new cars. We've been described as fanatics. We are. Our lives are dominated by one great, overshadowing factor—the struggle for socialism. Well, that's what my life is going to be. That's the black side of it. Then there is the other side of it. We Communists have a philosophy of life which no amount of money could buy. We have a cause to fight for, a definite purpose in life. We subordinate our petty personal selves into a great movement of humanity.

We have a morale, an *esprit de corps* such as no capitalist army ever had; we have a code of conduct, a way of life, a devotion to our cause that no religious order can touch. And we are guided not by blind, fanatical faith but by logic and reason, by a never-ending education of study and practice. And if our personal lives seem hard or our egos appear to suffer through subordination to the party, then we are adequately compensated by the thought that each of us is in his small way helping to contribute something new and true, something better to mankind."

That, unmistakably, is dedication to a cause. Substitute your own major goal in life for the words *Communist, Communism* and *Socialism* in this letter and you have some idea as to what total commitment means. Lack of application and effort keep many from real commitment, and real success is not possible until some form of genuine commitment has taken place. The successful man can actually visualize the goal which he has set for himself and "see" its fulfillment in advance.

Dr. Wallace A. Erickson, president of Wallace A. Erickson and Company and the Erickson Foundation in Chicago, defines success as "the progressive realization of a goal." The single-minded man will have a specific goal and will begin the task of realizing it the very moment he sets it.

As expressed by Paul J. Meyer of the Success Motivation Institute, "You can have anything you want in life when you crystallize your thinking. Actually, every step of progres since the world began has been taken because one man or one group of men realized that dedication, singleness of purpose, a magnificent obsession, the overpowering desire to accomplish one thing, was the only way to move forward."

Meyer added that "the totally committed man isn't hard to recognize; he stands head and shoulders above every crowd. He wears 'success blinders.' He looks neither to the right nor left, only straight ahead. He asks only for opportunity; he knows he can make the most of it. He doesn't want to hide in a sea of mediocrity, humbled and dulled by failure. He wants to dream, to build, to use his God-given imagination, to make mistakes, to learn and profit by those mistakes, and inevitably to succeed. He wants to live at the crest of the hill, to walk among the stars."

You can be that kind of person. And single-mindedness is one important step toward that accomplishment.

How To Be Single-minded

1. Take time to settle upon a single, specific, major goal for your life.
2. Gear your daily schedule to accomplish that purpose.
3. Discipline yourself to review that goal carefully at the beginning and conclusion of every day.
4. Read literature that will help toward fulfillment of that goal.
5. Associate as much as possible with those who enable you to fulfill your major purpose in life best.

Answer *yes* or *no*. Statements that are not applicable to your life on a specific day should not be counted in your score for that day. Eight or more *yes* answers: *superior;* six or seven, *excellent;* four or five, *good;* two or three, *fair;* one or none, *poor.*

1. In spite of a multitude of conflicting thoughts clamoring for attention, one overriding purpose remained uppermost as I proceeded into the day.
2. I did not allow the first unfavorable incident of the day to sidetrack me from my main goal.
3. A combination of several adverse circumstances failed to cause me to waver in my life purpose.
4. Even amidst many duties at the office (home, school), underneath and predominant was a single goal.
5. My televiewing today was not of the type that would completely erase and tear down the number one aim of my life.
6. I consciously kept in mind my major purpose in contacts with neighbors today—or in my thoughts about them.
7. Even my eating habits were influenced, if not controlled, by that primary goal which rules my life.
8. Exercise, rest and recreation came in proper balance to work toward better fulfillment of my aims.
9. Any radio listening I did did not deter or detract in the slightest from my major goal in life.
10. My devotional reading was read with a major purpose in mind.

SUCCESS DIARY

Week No. 3   Dates......................19...... to ....19......

Major Goal: Be Single-minded!
Minor Goal: Be Enthusiastic!

(Check appropriate scores for each day)

Achievement of Goals		Superior	Excellent	Good	Fair	Poor
Sunday	(Major)					
	(Minor)					
Monday	(Major)					
	(Minor)					
Tuesday	(Major)					
	(Minor)					
Wednesday	(Major)					
	(Minor)					
Thursday	(Major)					
	(Minor)					
Friday	(Major)					
	(Minor)					
Saturday	(Major)					
	(Minor)					

Remarks:

4.
Can I Really Stick to It?

THE ATHLETE who directed the 1963 National Football League championship team, the Chicago Bears, attributes his success in this rugged sport to *perseverance* as much as to skill. Quarterback Bill Wade of Nashville, Tennessee, told the authors:

Thirty years of competitive football have taught me many important lessons of life, but one which can be related to the subject of success very readily is the lesson of perseverance.

Whether a fellow plays in the back yard, on the streets or on the marked-off gridiron with an organized team, every football game is based upon the goal. The object is to score more points and thereby be declared victor. Paul wrote, "Know ye not that they which run in a race run all . . . ? So run that ye may obtain [the prize]" (I Corinthians 9:24).

. . . every life needs a never-changing goal, and I believe the life of Christ, His way, is the great supreme goal which we must persevere to attain. Disappointments, misunderstandings, heartache and heartbreak must never shield our view of the goal ahead which was marked off by the Master and remains constant on the field of life. As participants we must remain constant in our pursuit of perfection, with the willingness to accept our errors as part of the game. The loving Father already has provided forgiveness and in accepting that forgiveness we must do one thing: forgetting what lies behind, press toward the mark for the prize of the high calling of God in Christ Jesus. . . .

With this attitude, perseverance actually becomes the living expression of faith, that which drives a person onward in spite of circumstances.

This professional athlete, like many others, has found that the game of life, like the game of football, pays rich dividends for the one who perseveres. In the oft-quoted words of the late Dr. V. Raymond Edman, long-time President and later Chancellor of Wheaton College, and editor of *The Alliance Witness:* "It's always too soon to quit."

Many of America's great leaders, in various fields of endeavor, have learned this lesson. One in particular faced every conceivable obstacle in his upward climb. Here is his record:

1831, failed in business; 1832, defeated for the legislature; 1833, again failed in business; 1834, elected to legislature; 1835, sweetheart died; 1836, had a nervous breakdown; 1838, defeated for legislative speaker; 1840, defeated for elector; 1843, defeated for Congress; 1846, elected to Congress; 1848, defeated for Congress; 1855, defeated for Senate; 1856, defeated for Vice President; 1858, defeated for Senate. But in 1860 the record changed: he was *elected President!* Although he had many defeats, Abraham Lincoln considered them only temporary and he turned them into steppingstones to success. No doubt his sterling example affected many world figures in the century that followed.

After a heartbreaking series of experiments, Thomas A. Edison—the "Wizard of Menlo Park, New Jersey" —refused to become discouraged. "We haven't failed yet," he said to a co-worker. "We now know one thousand things that won't work, so we're that much closer to finding what will." Had he not persevered, one can only imagine the resultant developments in the fields of light and electricity, as well as in many other areas which would have felt the effect.

In more recent years, young Walter Judd faced heavy odds against him. He became self-conscious and depressed when a heavy dose of X rays scarred his face permanently, while he was undergoing treatment for acne. But Judd determined not to quit. "With God's help I'll do the best I can," he vowed. Walter Judd became an honored medical missionary to China and, in time, a distinguished Congressman, who served a record ten terms.

Napoleon Hill offers four practical suggestions for developing persistence: 1) a definite purpose backed by burning desire for its fulfillment; 2) a definite plan expressed in continuous action; 3) a mind closed tightly against all negative and discouraging influences, including negative suggestions of relatives, friends and acquaintances; 4) a friendly alliance with one or more persons who will encourage one to follow through with both plans and purpose. Many people in all walks of life have proved the truth of his assertion.

Although only five men had succeeded in swimming the English Channel, and she herself had failed twice,

Gertrude Ederle—renowned girl athlete—accomplished this feat in 1926 in fourteen hours and thirty-one minutes. Her record was two hours and twenty-three minutes faster than the best previous one, set in 1923 by male swimmer Charles Toth of Boston, Massachusetts. Three miles from her goal, cold, exhausted, battered, sickened by eleven hours of torture, she refused to heed the advice of her father and her trainer. When they asked her if she did not want to quit she responded with the classic retort, "Quit? What for?" That kind of never-say-die spirit has its parallel in almost every area of endeavor and, almost without exception, the results are predictable. *Perseverance pays off.*

Several years ago, New England industrialist F. Nelson Blount, owner of several small rail lines and founder of Steamtown, U.S.A., had an experience with perseverance—his own and that of a total stranger—that changed his whole life.

Blount, who was interested in several large firms went to Montreal on business, and was sitting in the lobby of the Queen Elizabeth Hotel when he met Chattanooga insurance executive Ted DeMoss, who was attending a convention of Christian Business Men's Committee International (of which he became International Chairman in 1968). DeMoss shared his faith with the wealthy New Englander, but seemed to get nowhere. He refused to drop the matter, however, and kept in touch with Blount through letters and long-distance phone calls. His persistence paid off when some weeks later the industrialist paid him a flying visit. Before the brief get-together in Chattanooga had ended, Blount had committed himself to a decision he perhaps least expected. In the following months, before he died in a plane accident in August, 1967, Blount spent a major portion of his time touring the country on speaking engagements, sharing the faith which had revolutionized his life. His experience is typical of many who have felt the impact of persistence.

Walter Knott, founder and owner of the famed Knott's Berry Farm in Buena Park, California, told the authors why he failed to attain certain goals in his successful career. "I simply was not willing to pay the price of concentrating, waiting, working, visualizing, planning, believing and persisting," he said. But one big, seemingly impractical dream did come to fulfillment for this man because he persevered in the face of overwhelming odds.

Long an admirer of Americana, Knott yearned to build an exact replica of Independence Hall on the Farm. Expense proved to be the first deterrent; then many problems arose in trying to copy a 230-year-old building: making 130,000 handmade bricks with fingerprints and a weathered appearance; plus a tower more than sixteen stories high; a great clock with four faces, ten feet across; an exact replica of the famed Liberty Bell. The "big, exciting and rewarding project," as Knott described it, came to a successful conclusion on July 4th, 1966. During the first two months, more than one hundred thousand people took the guided inspirational tour. A dream had come true, but not without hard work—and persistence.

The Waco success authority, Paul J. Meyer, points out that "it is a trait of human nature to try until your endurance runs out and then quit." But he adds these penetrating questions: "Have you ever measured your own powers of resistance; what does it take to defeat you? Do you know at what point on the barometer of buyer reluctance you begin to freeze in submission? How many times can you bounce back? There aren't enough 'no's' in any language to discourage the man who honestly wants to be a winner.''

One such man is Republican Congressman Glenn C. Cunningham of Nebraska who, in 1962, bucked the Justice, State and Post Office Departments, the White House, the Central Intelligence Agency and the United States Information Agency. Persistence paid off and Cunningham helped press through Congress the re-adoption of an amendment restoring government censorship of mail matter from abroad. The bill, aimed at stopping Communist propaganda from infiltrating the country, met with unexpected success. Why? Because a determined government servant refused to quit.

The history of the world is replete with stories of successful men—men who achieved their goals primarily because they wouldn't give up. Francois Pasqualini summed it up this way: ''The basic rules for success may be defined as follows: Know what you want. Find out what it takes to get it. Act on it. And persevere.''

How To Be Persevering

1. Have a definite plan for your life.
2. Couple it with a burning desire.
3. Let no obstacle, trial or tribulation—not even a brief detour—hinder you from pursuing your life's goal.
4. Cultivate friends and associates who will help you toward achievement of your goal. Avoid those who deter you from your goal.

Answer *yes* or *no*. Statements that are not applicable to your life on a specific day should not be counted in your score for that day. Eight or more *yes* answers: *superior;* six or seven, *excellent;* four or five, *good;* two or three, *fair;* one or none, *poor.*

1. My first project for the day (in the office, at home, in school) earned my steady attention until it was completed.
2. My family knows that determination and perseverance are qualities that have characterized my life this day.
3. Aches and pains failed to deter me in my specific duties for the day.
4. While sentiment might have led me to relax discipline in my own life as well as toward my loved ones, I persevered in what seemed right to me.
5. Although at times I was disillusioned by others, and tempted to withdraw from such wholesome activities as church boards and PTA, I continued to participate.
6. Encouragement in my chosen line of endeavor was clearly lacking today, but I persisted in doing that which I felt to be right.
7. Nothing deterred me from pursuing all of the details relative to my rightful duties for this day.
8. Despite a lack of genuine desire to continue my Bible reading and to pray, I stuck with it in the certain knowledge that it was the right thing to do.
9. When my devotional reading became difficult, I did not let it deter me from continuing and completing my usual assignment.
10. Today, I have kept in mind those deep spiritual desires which the Lord has impressed upon me.

SUCCESS DIARY

Week No. 4   Dates.....................19...... to ....19......

Major Goal: Be Persevering!
Minor Goal: Be Single-minded!

(Check appropriate scores for each day)

Achievement of Goals		Superior	Excellent	Good	Fair	Poor
Sunday	(Major)					
	(Minor)					
Monday	(Major)					
	(Minor)					
Tuesday	(Major)					
	(Minor)					
Wednesday	(Major)					
	(Minor)					
Thursday	(Major)					
	(Minor)					
Friday	(Major)					
	(Minor)					
Saturday	(Major)					
	(Minor)					

Remarks:

5.

Am I the Right Kind of Clock Watcher?

ALL OF US truly are born equal and we remain on an
equal footing throughout life, in one respect—the
amount of time allotted to each one of us. Every last
one of us has twenty-four hours to the day, 168 hours
to the week, fifty-two weeks to the year—no more, no
less. Here is an area where no one has an advantage
over us but, if we so choose, we may have an advantage
over most others.

How can we gain an advantage—not against others
but toward our specific goals in life—in this vital
area? *First,* we must be diligent not to waste any
time. We must watch over our time as we would over
a great treasure, which indeed is what our time represents. *Second,* we can put in more time at our God-
appointed tasks than do others. Let us assume that the
average person actually works six hours out of the
normal seven-and-a-half-hour working day. But you
and I can readily extend this to at least ten hours
if we really want to, and it is not at all difficult when
we are doing the job God called us to and we are really
doing it for Him.

In fact, once we ascertain God's will for our life and
not only get in it but get *caught up* in it, it is harder
to stop after ten hours than to keep going. Now we

love *what* we are doing and we love doing it because we love the One for whom we are doing it. When we are co-laborers together with God we are not going to be clock watchers. Nor will we, like the average American, spend more time each week before a television set than on the job. (Yes, hard as it is to believe, a recent survey showed that the average American spends forty-two hours a week watching TV!)

So, working a ten-hour day will give us a big advantage over the average person. The effect of this, compounded over a period of time, becomes astronomical. Try it for a while and see! It is amazing how many people, who are careful and frugal with dollars and even pennies, shamelessly waste time, with no apparent concern or realization that time is actually money —it is our time, after all, which we exchange for money. Waste of time is probably worse than waste of money for, while the latter usually can be made up, time lost can never be recouped.

One specific way most of us can utilize our time better is to carry along some reading matter or a project that requires some additional time. What better way to capitalize on odd moments between planes, trains and appointments; waiting for someone, or if we become stranded somewhere unexpectedly?

Granted, this type of extra effort is not expected of most of us. Yet herein lies one of the secrets of leadership and success—doing *more* than is expected of us, *more* than we are paid to do. Remember, cream always rises to the top and so does quality. And going the second mile, *giving* more than we get, is one of the touchstones of quality.

Planning your time is absolutely essential to achieve any degree of success. We do not need more hours, we need proper planning of the hours we do have. As someone once said, you can lose your wealth and by work and economy get it back. But whoever heard of anyone recovering one hour of lost time?

Paul J. Meyer suggests four ways to squeeze an extra hour into every day: 1) save your time for something special; 2) chart your time to locate time leaks; 3) organize your time to plug the leaks; 4) think about time all the time. "A calendar and a clock only measure the passage of time," he said. "They can't mark the difference that gives one man time to spare while another man never has time enough. No matter how young or old you are at this particular moment, time is on your side. Your greatest asset in achieving whatever you desire in life lies in learning how to organize your time."

Meyer has a five-part plan for time organization: 1) define your goal; 2) create a timetable for each step; 3) do only one thing at a time; 4) ask how much your time is worth; 5) ask what is really essential. "Two principal methods of beating time are already practiced by progressive executives," he said. "The first of these is selectivity. The second method is delegation." He added this succinct rule of thumb: "You can't master your time until you master yourself."

Six steps toward mastering time also come from the creative genius of this Texas executive: make notes; remove distractions from your work area; discourage interruptions; learn to say "no"; learn to listen carefully; let the postman be your errand boy.

Ralph Waldo Emerson had his own words of wisdom on the subject of time: "Finish each day and be done with it; tomorrow is a new day." And Horace Mann once remarked: "Lost, yesterday somewhere between sunrise and sunset, two golden hours, each set with sixty diamond minutes. No reward is offered, for they are gone forever."

According to sociologist Robert K. Merton, who wrote on the development of Western technology and science, John Calvin's emphasis on the stewardship and value of time triggered the watch industry in Geneva, Switzerland, which, in turn, ushered in the whole modern era of technology and industry.

A strong believer in the value of time, Benjamin Franklin made full use of his minutes and hours. Like anthropologist John Mason, he believed that "as every thread of gold is valuable, so is every moment of time." One day, a customer came into Franklin's little bookstore in Philadelphia to buy a book. Not satisfied with the asking price, he asked to see the proprietor.

"Mr. Franklin is very busy," the clerk said. But the customer, who had spent an hour thumbing through the books, insisted and Ben Franklin responded to the call and confronted the unhappy customer.

"What is the lowest price you can take for this book?" the customer inquired.

"A dollar and a quarter," Franklin replied.

"A dollar and a quarter! Your clerk asked me for only a dollar."

"True," Franklin countered, "and I could have better afforded to take a dollar than to leave my work."

The customer, not quite sure whether the proprietor was joking, pursued the matter further. "Come now," he said, "tell me your lowest price for the book."

"A dollar and a half," Franklin replied.

"A dollar and a half! Why, you just offered it for a dollar and a quarter."

"Yes," the wily proprietor concluded, "and I could

better have taken that price than a dollar and a half now.''

Surely that extreme consciousness of the value of time must have had some relation to the accomplishments of the man. And thus it is today. The late T. E. McCully, for many years a baking executive in Milwaukee, before he became executive secretary of Christian Business Men's Committee International, had a fruitful ministry during his ten years with the organization.

When McCully's son Ed, with four of his colleagues, met death at the hands of the Auca Indians in the jungles of Ecuador in January, 1956, a divine compulsion came upon the bereaved father. He determined not only to ''do the works of his Father who sent him,'' but to redouble his efforts in order to compensate for the time and effort his son might have given had he lived. Hundreds of lives, including those of many young people, found new meaning and purpose as a result of McCully's effective witness. And it all stemmed from a new realization of the preciousness of time.

Executive Editor Wayne Christianson, of *Moody Monthly* magazine, had a divinely inspired treatise on the subject, ''Five Minutes After,'' that has been widely discussed and reprinted because of its thought-provoking truths:

It may be in a moment, or after months of waiting, but soon I shall stand before my Lord—perhaps even before the year is over. Then, in an instant, all things will appear in a new perspective. The things I thought important—tomorrow's tasks, my success or failure in pleasing those around me—will not matter at all. And the things to which I gave but little thought—the word about Christ to the man next door, the moment (how short it was!) of earnest prayer for the Lord's work in faroff lands, the confessing and forsaking of that secret sin—will stand as real and enduring.

Five minutes after I'm in heaven, I'll be overwhelmed by the truth I've known but somehow never grasped. I'll realize then that it's what I am in Christ that comes first with God and that when I am right with Him I do the things that please. Him. I'll sense that it was not just how much I gave that mattered, but how I gave and how much I withheld.

In heaven I'll wish with all my heart that I could reclaim a thousandth part of the time that I've let slip through my fingers, that I could call back those countless conversations which could have glorified my Lord, but didn't. Five minutes after I'm in heaven I believe I'll wish with all my heart that I had risen more faithfully to read the Word of God and wait on Him in prayer . . . that I might have known Him here on earth as He wanted me to know Him.

A thousand thoughts will press upon me, and, though overwhelmed by the grace which admits me to my heavenly home, I'll wonder at my aimless earthly life: I'll wish (if one may wish in heaven) . . . but it will be too late! Heaven is real and hell is real and eternity is but a breath away. Soon we shall be in the presence of the Lord we claim to serve. Why should we live as though salvation were a dream—as though we did not know? "To him that knoweth to do good, and doeth it not, to him it is sin." There may yet be a little time. God help us to live *now* in the light of that real tomorrow.

As an unknown poet once wrote:

He was going to be all mortal should be—
    tomorrow.
No one should be kinder nor braver than he—
    tomorrow.
A friend who was troubled and weary he knew,
Who'd be glad of a light and who needed it, too.
On him he would call and see what he could do—
    tomorrow.

Each morning he stacked up the letters he'd write—
    tomorrow.
And thought of the folks he'd fill with delight—
    tomorrow.
It was too bad, indeed, he was busy today,
And hadn't a minute to stop on the way;
More time he'd have to give others, he'd say—
    tomorrow.

The greatest of workers this man would have been—
    tomorrow.
The world would have known him had he ever seen
    tomorrow.
But the fact is, he died and he faded from view,
And all that he left here when living was through
Was a mountain of things he intended to do—
    tomorrow.

1. Be time conscious.
2. Establish your priorities in life.
3. Budget your time so as to effect a minimum of wasted hours.
4. Carry a pad and pencil, reading matter, and portable dictating machine with you for use in spare moments.
5. Determine to live every moment in the light of eternity.

Am I the Right Kind of Clock Watcher?

Answer *yes* or *no*. Statements that are not applicable to your life on a specific day should not be counted in your score for that day. Eight or more *yes* answers: *superior;* six or seven, *excellent;* four or five, *good;* two or three, *fair;* one or none, *poor.*

1. Realizing the value of spending each hour of the day and night wisely, including time for sleep, I gave my body the amount of rest I knew it needed.
2. Aware that every moment is precious, I arose at an hour that allowed ample time to prepare properly for the day.
3. I have been aware during the day that minutes were flying by that could never be regained.
4. As I read newspapers and magazines, I was conscious that this was time that needed to be measured carefully and not wasted.
5. My glances at the clock today came from a consciousness of the value of each moment.
6. I did not spend time with meaningless television programs.

7. Any time I spent with the radio came about because of a desire to keep up with world news or to hear some message of importance to my well-being.

8. I recognized the truth of the assertion that each one of us has time sufficient to do anything he wants to do badly enough.

9. The truth of the Scriptural injunction to "redeem the time" has not been lost upon me today.

10. Knowing that all time rightly belongs to God, I gave Him back part of my time in His Word and prayer.

SUCCESS DIARY

Week No. 5   Dates.................19...... to ....19......

Major Goal: Be Time-Conscious!
Minor Goal: Be Persevering!

(Check appropriate scores for each day)

Achievement of Goals		Superior	Excellent	Good	Fair	Poor
Sunday	(Major)					
	(Minor)					
Monday	(Major)					
	(Minor)					
Tuesday	(Major)					
	(Minor)					
Wednesday	(Major)					
	(Minor)					
Thursday	(Major)					
	(Minor)					
Friday	(Major)					
	(Minor)					
Saturday	(Major)					
	(Minor)					

Remarks:

6.

Do I Roll with the Punch?

You CAN call the trait flexibility, adjustability or whatever you will, but without it you will be hard-pressed to achieve a measurable amount of success. Such adjustability is rewarding in every line of endeavor and can make one not only an agreeable companion and colaborer but—more important—a more effective person. Certainly it smoothes the pathway along life's journey and oils the creaky joints of human temperament that can prove to be real stumbling blocks in the upward climb toward success if they are left unchecked.

This kind of adjustability requires an open-mindedness, a willingness to listen to others and to learn. Sometimes pride can bring about a certain rigidity that makes one afraid to admit a mistake; afraid to expand, to cut back or to change course as circumstances might seem to dictate. Flexibility presupposes, then, a degree of humility in sizing up facts and facing them honestly.

When the Bible suggests that we should "in everything give thanks," it is more than just an exercise in words; it is, in fact, a practical step that eases the path toward success. We can learn something from every experience of life—the good and the bad. When adversity strikes, we should look for some lesson that can be harnessed for our benefit. There is nothing that happens to us that cannot be turned into our gain.

Dr. Richard C. Halverson, a Washington, D. C., minister who is active in International Christian Leadership—sponsors of the annual Presidential Prayer Breakfast—tells of two words which express profoundly the "bankruptcy of so much effort"—*always* and *never*.

" 'We've never done it that way before.' For many otherwise intelligent and reasonable people, that explanation is enough to sidetrack any good idea at any time under any circumstances," Halverson said. "Dismissing every new or unconventional idea with such 'logic' has become a habit with many. 'We have never. . . .' That settles it! No wonder their organization has become an ingrown—sterile—mutual admiration society busy about nothing except its own preservation. 'We have *always* done it this way.' Who can measure the incalculable loss of influence . . . because there were those in leadership who simply refused to think beyond the old, established, innocuous patterns."

The practicality of flexibility can be established quickly by taking a bird's eye view of the average home and observing the family's initial reaction to difficult situations that arise. It is Saturday morning, and Father has planned an early round of golf. He awakens and rolls out of bed to the rumble of thunder, punctuated by jagged streaks of lightning. The faint pitter-patter of rain becomes a torrential downpour in a matter of moments. Father buries his head in his hands; his day is ruined.

Mother too awakens with big plans for the day: laundry, grocery shopping, ironing, housecleaning, beauty parlor—the completion of which always brings a warm sense of accomplishment. A weak but painful cry from Junior's bedroom interrupts her reverie. One touch of his forehead reveals the awful truth; he has a raging fever. Mother finds it difficult to shift mental gears to meet the forced change in the day's schedule. Or take the case of daughter, who can hardly wait for her big Saturday-night date. Barely has breakfast been completed when the phone rings; regretfully, Mr. Big cancels their date. The blow is a major one for her.

Rightfully, of course, none of these events could be considered a major crisis in the life of the family. But each one becomes serious because of the way it affects the individual involved. Flexibility—adjustability— has not been learned with sufficient thoroughness to "roll with the punch" and come up smiling. But, with daily training, it is possible to learn how to bounce back and adjust to the situation. It is not so much what happens to us that affects our lives—it is the way we react to that which happens to us. As someone once said: What we are eating is not nearly so important to our physical welfare as what is eating us.

Take the case of the executive who arrives at the office in an uneasy mood. His repartee with the family at breakfast set the pattern and he left home without mending fences. Now he finds it difficult, if not impossible, to overlook the behavioral flaws of his business associates. The very quality of adjustability that he considers essential in his employees is lacking in his own life at the moment. Nerves are on edge and tempers threaten to flare as the day progresses.

The same situation can prevail at school. The student arrives in an agreeable mood, only to find in his first class that his teacher has concocted a difficult test, on the spur of the moment. Caught offguard, the student fails to respond properly and not only ruins his whole day but earns a nonpassing grade on his test.

Such lack of adjustment can bring the wheels of progress almost to a standstill. Some give up, crack up or drop out, while others learn to adjust. Suppose your heart is set on a certain plan, a particular mate, a pet project or even a life career, when plans are interrupted by sickness, the wise counsel of others or just plain lack materialization. *Then* is the time to have an attentive ear, a flexible heart and mind. Possibly a better plan or course or choice will evolve. It is no time for rigidity, inflexibility, intransigence, closed-mindedness—all of which are very costly to our pursuit of success. These traits will restrict our potential, by confining us to our limited spheres of knowledge, experience and wisdom and will cut us off from the help and counsel which others can—and frequently will—contribute. Being a good listener is a rare and valuable trait.

Is there any cure, any real solution for the problem of stubbornness in such matters? Yes, daily progress can be made in this vital realm with the help of a "Million Dollar Secret"—an important first step toward genuine flexibility—that has paved the way for the authors and many others, in the realm of goodwill and human relations. One Maryland octogenarian, after hearing about the formula, commented: "Oh, how I wish I had realized the truth of that counsel eighty years ago! My, how different my life would have been!" Here, briefly, is the "Million Dollar Secret," so-called because strict adherence to it is worth far more than that amount in providing an easy conscience and great inner peace for the one who practices it on a regular basis:

Never say a single word of any kind to an associate, employer, employee, neighbor or member of your own family until first you have assured yourself in your own mind and heart that what you are about to say is to be said in love.

Apply that same principle to the war in Viet Nam, racial tensions, international affairs, and whatever else comes to your mind, and you will see that the ramifications are immense. In our immediate context, adherence to this principle will constitute a giant step toward genuine success that cannot be gainsaid. It is impossible to overemphasize the importance of adjustability. Begin now to cultivate it; consciously and deliberately determine to utilize the "Million Dollar Secret" in every area of your life. And if what you say is said in love, you will be able to take the matter of flexibility seriously. Then watch the miracles take place.

How To Be Flexible

1. Practice the art of adjusting to situations of all kinds.
2. Cultivate alertness and sensitivity to an inner voice that often gives an indication of things to come.
3. Consciously practice the Golden Rule in your daily associations with others.
4. Be not only willing, but eager to adjust to the varying circumstances of the day.
5. Make full use of the "Million Dollar Secret" at every possible opportunity.

Answer *yes* or *no*. Statements that are not applicable to your life on a specific day should not be counted in your score for that day. Eight or more *yes* answers: *superior;* six or seven, *excellent;* four or five, *good;* two or three, *fair;* one or none, *poor.*

1. At the first necessary change in my scheduled plans for the day I reacted well.
2. When my viewpoint was challenged I received the suggestions amicably.
3. When a favorite program on television was preempted by a news special it did not disturb my equilibrium.
4. Upsets in the schedule of my children during the day did not ruffle me unduly.
5. That first project at the office (cleaning program in the home, or exam at school) failed to throw me even though it was far from what I expected.
6. When my stubbornness brought about an impasse in relations with others, I relented and tried to mend fences and heal grievances.
7. Events fluctuated to an extent I had not expected, but I rearranged my schedule accordingly.
8. One of my best friends disappointed me, but I recovered from the blow and followed through with my plans for the day.
9. World conditions, though steadily worsening, failed to fluster me in my determination to press toward my goal.
10. When my reading in the Bible disproved some beliefs I had held I adjusted gladly to the truth of the Word.

SUCCESS DIARY

Week No. 6   Dates.....................19...... to ....19......

Major Goal: Be Flexible!
Minor Goal: Be Time-Conscious!

(Check appropriate scores for each day)

Achievement of Goals		Superior	Excellent	Good	Fair	Poor
Sunday	(Major)					
	(Minor)					
Monday	(Major)					
	(Minor)					
Tuesday	(Major)					
	(Minor)					
Wednesday	(Major)					
	(Minor)					
Thursday	(Major)					
	(Minor)					
Friday	(Major)					
	(Minor)					
Saturday	(Major)					
	(Minor)					

Remarks:

7.
How Sure Am I?

SOMEONE has defined *confidence* as the thing that enables you to eat blackberry jam at a picnic without looking to see if the seeds move. But Emerson declared: "They conquer who believe they can. He has not learned the lesson of life who does not each day surmount a fear." In both cases confidence comes from a right attitude.

That kind of attitude works in the athletic realm as well. For Don Shinnick, All-pro linebacker for the Baltimore Colts of the National Football League, confidence is an absolute essential in his chosen profession. "In any business," Shinnick told the authors, "you have to have 100 percent confidence in your ability to get the job done. This is certainly true in my job. There are many things that make an individual confident. Two things, in particular, are very important: knowing your opponent's weaknesses and strong points, and knowing your own weaknesses and strong points. By knowing these things you can adjust to different situations. You won't be surprised at any development. In most cases you will come out on top."

Shinnick added: "In my Christian life too I find this to be true. The Lord wants us to be confident in what we do. We should know our opponent, the devil—his strong points and his weak points. We should know our own, too, and depend upon the Lord to help us in every situation.''

Another professional athlete, pitcher Don Sutton of the Los Angeles Dodgers, echoed Shinnick's views. ''When I am on the mound I have to be cocky,'' the twenty-two-year-old rookie told us. ''A good competitor must have something of a 'red-neck' attitude between the white lines.''

The kind of confidence needed is best exemplified by the younger generation. One day a small boy played calmly on the deck of a storm-tossed ship, ignoring the upheaval around him. Sitting in a sheltered recess of the deck, which afforded protection from the fury of the wind, the lad was oblivious to the fearful passengers who gazed upon him through the portholes of their staterooms. Finally, one deeply concerned passenger called to the boy above the sound of the howling winds. ''Son,'' he shouted, ''aren't you afraid of the storm? Don't you think you should come inside?'' The boy looked up momentarily, smiled and replied, ''Oh, no, I'm not afraid. My father's the captain!''

One person who admittedly wants to be a man of great confidence is thirty-three-year-old Wendell Nance, founder and president of Wendell Nance and Associates, who teaches motivational and sales techniques and is in such demand that in a recent twelve-month period he held more than a hundred leadership and sales workshops. ''In most people,'' he declared, ''a lot of what passes for humility is nothing but fear. But God hasn't given us the spirit of fear.'' The alternative, of course, is a spirit of confidence—the glorious possibility for all who would meet the conditions.

Don Jennings, writing in the *Prairie Farmer*,

summed up the subject well: "There are many words that give expression of our attitude toward life. There is one without which our entire future would limp. That one word is confidence. In early childhood it makes us brave; in youth it gives us courage; as adults it makes the necessary loads easier to bear; on the sunset trail of age it lights our pathway down the valley of uncertainty."

The real secret of having confidence and being able to express it lies in the source of our assurance. As he lay on his deathbed, the great scientist, Michael Faraday was asked, "What are your speculations now?" His reply was quick and confident: "I have no speculations; I *know* whom I have believed!"

That kind of confidence has buoyed many men in all walks of life. A Milwaukee attorney, Paul Konnor, once a Golden Gloves boxing champion and a member of Colonel William "Lucky" Darby's famed Rangers during World War II, experienced danger and fear when he and his buddies fell into a German trap. But a later incident gave him confidence that displayed itself often along his life's pathway, and has continued through the years.

Riding Flight 83 from Chicago, Konnor realized the jet was in trouble. Instead of landing at Miami International Airport the plane shifted course abruptly and headed out over the cold Atlantic, hastily releasing its excess fuel. "Fasten seatbelts and prepare for emergency landing!" Sharp fear and sudden tension swept over the passengers. One notable exception brought a shrill yell: "Wake that man up! He must be told what is about to happen to us!" Konnor opened his eyes. "I haven't been asleep," he said calmly. "And if I appear unconcerned it's because long ago

I placed my future in the secure hands of my Lord and Saviour, Jesus Christ.''

That kind of confidence is rare, but possible to all. An expert in the sales field suggests at least five important factors that go into the attainment of confidence. Paul J. Meyer encourages his clients to adopt this positive attitude: "Believe in yourself. Believe that it's impossible for you to make a mistake, regardless of any situation's outcome. Consider every human error as a lesson, a steppingstone forward. With such a positive attitude there's only one way to go—*up*. If you misjudge a prospect's reaction and because of this lose a sale, think of it as a wonderful opportunity in adding to your knowledge of people.

"You learn by action, not by theory. When you've aimed towards a high personal goal, and you're temporarily thrown off course, an attitude of positive expectancy will bring your built-in correction mechanism into play and you'll be back on course again. Remember, with a positive mental attitude you are goal-directed and the inexorable Law of Attraction is working in your favor. You're a goer, you're a doer, you accomplish things.''

In his business of motivating people to their full potential Meyer tells them that "if you want people to respond when you call them on the phone, if you want to get action, then you will never do it by driving yourself. You must be driven. You must be driven by an idea a whole lot bigger than just the money you are going to get. You must be driven with an insatiable desire to see people unfold and be their better selves so they can live a more prosperous, happy, exciting and fruitful life. We must recognize that the only way to accomplish this is to change the way that people think.

"This kind of creative intangible selling can never be done on the intellectual level alone. People are moved by emotion. We have to understand this. We have to believe it and we have to act on it." Meyer also lists five motivational blocks to the type of confidence needed by every person who would be truly a success: low self-concept; reliving past failures; complacency; negative habit patterns, and low achievement drive.

Another way to acquire the kind of confidence that leads to real success is revealed by Aldous Huxley, the English novelist and essayist: "There's only one corner of the universe you can be certain of improving; that's your own self." As surely as this improvement begins to take place, confidence asserts itself because it has some foundation in fact. Thinking well of oneself is not all wrong, for "as a man thinketh in his heart, so is he." We must have confidence in ourselves even while paradoxically we recognize that the only good thing about any person is the Lord Jesus Christ. Let us never underestimate ourselves, for we are "fearfully and wonderfully made"—God's handiwork.

T. J. Watson, Jr., Chairman and Chief Executive Officer of IBM (International Business Machines), is a firm believer in the importance of confidence. "The men who set out to do what others say cannot be done are the ones who make the discoveries, produce the inventions and move the world ahead. Believing in success can help to make it so."

A Christian leader of the past said it in another way: "We don't test the resources of God until we attempt the impossible," declared F. B. Meyer.

Echoing a similar sentiment is Evangelist John Haggai of Atlanta, Ga., who said: "Attempt something so impossible that unless God is in it it's doomed to failure."

How To Be Confident

1. Know your own weaknesses and strengths.
2. Know the weaknesses and strengths of your competition or opposition.
3. Know where your confidence lies; on whom it is based.
4. Realize that a mistake or an error is only a new opportunity to learn.

How Sure Am I?

Answer *yes* or *no*. Statements that are not applicable to your life on a specific day should not be counted in your score for that day. Eight or more *yes* answers: *superior;* six or seven, *excellent;* four or five, *good;* two or three, *fair;* one or none, *poor*.

1. I approached the day with the conviction that the world, in general, was on my side rather than against me.
2. I have fully recognized my weaknesses, but have allowed them to help rather than hinder my progress today.
3. Though conscious of my strong points I have not rested on my oars but have put out full effort in all I have undertaken.
4. The fact that I recognized the weaknesses of others did not cause me to lose a proper degree of confidence in them.

5. Though conscious of the strong points of others I did not let myself be unduly influenced by them.
6. Even though today was more successful than my ordinary day I did not let it cause my confidence to be placed in the wrong place.
7. Today I resisted the urge to place confidence in others than the Creator.
8. I have realized today the truth of the Word that any ability is that which God gives (I Peter 4:11).
9. As the day came to an end I could sincerely praise the Lord that my confidence had been in Him.
10. My future outlook is confident because of the One in whom I have placed my confidence.

SUCCESS DIARY

Week No. 7   Dates.....................19...... to ....19......

Major Goal: Be Confident!
Minor Goal: Be Flexible!

(Check appropriate scores for each day)

Achievement of Goals		Superior	Excellent	Good	Fair	Poor
Sunday	(Major)					
	(Minor)					
Monday	(Major)					
	(Minor)					
Tuesday	(Major)					
	(Minor)					
Wednesday	(Major)					
	(Minor)					
Thursday	(Major)					
	(Minor)					
Friday	(Major)					
	(Minor)					
Saturday	(Major)					
	(Minor)					

Remarks:

8.
Can I Take It?

THE FACULTY of being tough and *resilient* is important and effective along the road to success. The ability to face up to criticism—constructive and otherwise—has its inevitable rewards. Learning to take all barbs, insults, taunts and derisions as chariots that can draw you closer to your goal is real victory, for it is one more vital link in the long chain called success. Stubbornness, intractability, unyieldingness and irascibility are not a part of resiliency, which entails the possession and utilization of a thick skin when it counts.

Resilience must begin in the home, for it is there that the greatest tests frequently come. To properly discipline children, for example, requires a firmness and stick-to-it-iveness that is not easily moved by beautiful blue eyes and a sweet disposition brought into play to help counteract misbehavior. Young people and children, on the other hand, can display this same wonderful quality of rebounding by refusing to let punishment —just or unjust—get them down. The truth of the matter is that very few, if any, members of the human race escape some unjust treatment. Acceptance of this fact can help toward development of a healthy disposition that majors in resiliency.

It is in the home—among the people we actually

love the most, and vice versa—that thoughtless and unkind remarks demand a perceptive insight and a basic realization that the words of the old song are true: "You always hurt the one you love—the one you love most of all." Understanding this, and developing a forgiving spirit and a rhinoceros hide, along with a controlled tongue, help immensely toward paving the road to success.

The kind of toughness and resilience we have in mind is more a defensive weapon than an offensive one, for if it becomes the latter it is too easily wielded to harm and to hurt rather than to heal and to mend. Paradoxically, it *is* possible to combine the gentleness of the Psalmist—". . . thy gentleness hath made thee great" (18:35)—with the kind of quality we refer to in this chapter and emerge with a Christlike spirit that remains consistent.

This matter of resilience must be practiced not only at home but also at the office, the shop and the plant; at school and in the church; at work and at play. We must acquire the ability to take it, if the frustrations of our everyday circumstances are not to engulf us and thwart our efforts toward achievement of worthwhile goals. In the office, for example, any number of things can go wrong—change of plans, broken schedules, "people" problems, and a host of other setbacks. At the shop, unexpected absences, labor problems, major accidents—any number of things—can threaten to upset the smooth operation of the business. The employer or employee or foreman who remains resilient learns to accept such inevitabilities philosophically.

At school, perhaps the toughest discipline to learn is that of performing your work solely on your own. When all around you join the growing band of cheaters, it is not easy to stand boldly for old-fashioned, "square" honesty and decency, but it is one sure attribute along the road to genuine success. Apart from the moral implications, one can hardly expect to learn all that is expected of him if he is content to rely on others for his answers. It may be easier to follow the crowd—at exam time or at income tax time—but it is far more rewarding to stand firmly on principle and refuse to follow the crowd that wanders merrily along the road to mediocrity.

One of the most difficult areas of a right response reacting resiliently has to do with the spoken word. How easy it is to react violently to a word uttered "out of season"; how difficult it is to act properly under all circumstances, including those times when the bitter or harsh word comes forth. Only strong determination, properly meshed with a Christlike spirit and empowered with love by the Almighty Himself, can enable us to avoid reacting. But this restraint is another landmark along the thorn-strewn pathway leading to success and happiness. Failure to control the tongue can undo all kinds of good and can "sink ships," as the old saying goes.

Faith that God is still on His throne, that He rules and overrules in the affairs of men, is a necessary factor in this vital quality of resiliency. For without this assurance one might find it hard to accept the truth that Paul shared with the people of Rome so many years ago: "And we know that all things work together for good to them that love God, to them who are the called according to his purpose" (Romans 8:28). If one can—by blind faith, if necessary—accept the truth of this Scriptural principle, he can cushion himself against the blows of life that surely must fall ere we leave the earthly scene.

How resilient are you? Watch yourself the next time you are "thrown a curve" or caught offguard. If your first inclination is to react rather than to act, consider yourself perfectly normal—"par for the course." But, if you can disregard your natural inclinations in favor of discreet silence or positive action, you will have chalked up a real milestone in your career. And you will be able to go from victory to victory, finding it easier to bounce back at every turn and to make the most of any and all setbacks and disturbances. Forewarned is forearmed. Let's keep our moral armor sharpened and ready for every contingency at all times.

How To Be Resilient

1. Accept all insults and taunts as something more than mere derogatory remarks aimed at you personally.
2. Remember to act rather than react under all circumstances and in all situations; act as you know you should rather than as your old nature would have you do.
3. Be sensitive to the still, small voice of the Holy Spirit rather than to the unfeeling remarks of friend or foe.
4. As a Christian who, by faith is dead to sin and alive to God—as a "dead" man—refuse to acknowledge the disparaging remarks of others as insults and taunts.

Can I Take It?

Answer *yes* or *no*. Statements that are not applicable to your life on a specific day should not be counted in your score for that day. Eight or more *yes* answers: *superior;* six or seven, *excellent;* four or five, *good;* two or three, *fair;* one or none, *poor.*

1. I remembered to act rather than react under almost every circumstance that I encountered.

2. A thoughtless word aimed specifically in my direction failed to ruffle me.

3. I realized the truth of the assertion that "sticks and stones may break my bones, but names can never hurt me."

4. My own opinion about the character and ability of others was not influenced by what I felt they thought about me.

5. Realizing that "we always hurt the one we love," I proceeded as if certain things had not been said by my own loved ones.

6. The mail brought news that normally would have upset my equilibrium, but I took it as a character-building experience.

7. I overheard unfavorable comment about myself, but refused to take it too seriously or to let it upset me.

8. A radio or television commentator gave vent to strong language in references that might easily have been describing my own weaknesses, but I held my emotions well in check.

9. I was able to bring into subjection every thought of real or supposed feelings of resentment against me that stemmed from remarks made last Sunday.

10. My devotional reading for the day proved hard-hitting and particularly directed to me, it seemed, but I took it all in stride.

SUCCESS DIARY

Week No. 8   Dates...................19...... to ....19......

Major Goal: Be Resilient!
Minor Goal: Be Confident!

(Check appropriate scores for each day)

Achievement of Goals		Superior	Excellent	Good	Fair	Poor
Sunday	(Major) (Minor)					
Monday	(Major) (Minor)					
Tuesday	(Major) (Minor)					
Wednesday	(Major) (Minor)					
Thursday	(Major) (Minor)					
Friday	(Major) (Minor)					
Saturday	(Major) (Minor)					

Remarks:

9.

How Is My Get-up-and-go?

IF ONE HUMAN characteristic could describe best the secret of success achieved by Texas industrialist R. G. LeTourneau, it would have to be *hard work*. Far beyond retirement age, the near-octogenarian still continues a fantastic schedule that leaves many younger men gasping for breath along the way. Not content with his twelve- to fifteen-hour-a-day performance at the LeTourneau Company plant in Longview, Texas, the genial inventor-manufacturer also maintained weekend speaking schedules that reached many thousands of people.

Business and government leaders have widely acclaimed LeTourneau as one of the great manufacturers of all time. During World War II his machines built the Burma Road and cleared the Pacific atolls, and his firm got most of the armed forces' orders for the big bulldozers. Some consider him to be to the field of earth-moving machinery what the Wright Brothers were to the airplane industry.

To achieve such a reputation LeTourneau has manifested certain characteristics in his life from his earliest years: complete absorption in the task at hand, persistence, inquisitiveness, restlessness. When someone said a thing couldn't be done, usually that was the thing he set out to do. Perhaps his philosophy is expressed best by this sign, which hangs in his office: "According to the theory of aerodynamics, and as may be readily demonstrated through laboratory tests and wind-tunnel experiments, the bumblebee is unable to fly. This is because the size, weight and shape of his body, in relation to the total wingspread, makes flying impossible. But the bumblebee, being ignorant of these profound scientific truths, goes ahead and flies anyway, and manages to make a little honey every day."

A successful inventor and an energetic worker, LeTourneau has not always been considered a complete success as a business man, but he has employed others qualified in the field of business management to make up for his lack, and his industriousness has made him a living legend in the world of manufacturing. He is a man who agrees unequivocally with Kenneth Taylor's interpretation of the Proverbs in *Living Psalms and Proverbs:* "Lazy men are soon poor; hard workers get rich" (10:4); "Work hard and become a leader; be lazy and never succeed" (12:24); "Lazy people want much but get little, while the diligent are prospering" (13:4).

Two leading proponents of success make a strong point with which LeTourneau certainly would agree. Napoleon Hill and W. Clement Stone, in their book *Success Through a Positive Mental Attitude,* declare that "anything in life worth having is worth working for!" And Goethe observed that "energy will accomplish everything possible. No array of talents, circumstances or opportunities will make a two-legged animal a man without it." Someone else phrased it this way: "A man can accomplish anything with work; he can get nowhere without it."

Mary Kaiser, mother of the late Henry J. Kaiser, once said to her son: "If I leave you nothing else but the will to work, I will have left you the priceless gift: the joy of work. Loving people and serving them is the greatest value in life." What a far cry from today's something-for-nothing philosophy that seems to have captured much of society.

Automobile pioneer Henry Ford once declared that "the man who will use his skill and constructive imagination to see how much he can give for a dollar instead of how little he can give for a dollar is bound to succeed."

In a similar vein Eddie Rickenbacker told the authors: "One of our greatest blessings under the American Constitution is our right and freedom to work wherever we wish to, and at whatever we desire." It has been well said that, while the devil tempts every man, the idle man tempts the devil.

Ford Mason, the gumball machine magnate, learned the lesson early in life: "I was always an ambitious boy. I did not like idleness. I earned my first watch at the age of eleven or twelve through securing subscriptions to what was then called the *Mothers Magazine*. I learned early in my childhood that if I wanted anything worthwhile I had to work for it."

B. C. Brodie, echoing similar sentiments, observed that "nothing in this world is as good as usefulness. It binds your fellow creatures to you and you to them; it tends to the improvement of your own character and gives you a real importance in society, much beyond what any artificial station can bestow."

Even the man who relies on his Creator for help realizes he also has a part to play in the accomplishment of his goals. "Uncle Dan," a man said one day,

"I heard that you asked the Lord for that good garden. Is that correct?" "Yes, sir," proudly replied the man whose beautiful garden was his delight, "only I never pray for a good garden unless I have a hoe in my hand. I say, 'Lord, you send the sunshine and the rain and I'll keep down those weeds.'"

Such an attitude is not thinking small. As Pascal expressed it: "Always keep your eyes open for the little tasks, because it is the little task that is important to Jesus Christ. The future of the Kingdom of God does not depend on the enthusiasm of this or that powerful person; those great ones are necessary too, but it is equally necessary to have a great number of little people who will do a little thing in the service of Christ."

Whoever said, "The man who goes through life hunting for a soft thing can find it right under his hat," gave a timely reminder for today's ne'er-do-well, who would accumulate as much money for as little actual work as possible. Little does this ne'er-do-well realize the value of industriousness as a tool against involvement in evil.

The archer fish, found in East Indian waters, is a curious little fish that hunts its prey like a modern Polaris submarine. It gets its food by ejecting tiny drops of water from its mouth with terrific force. With deadly accuracy it can hit an insect some twenty inches or more away. Insects which rest on the surface of the water are favorite targets, as are those on branches hanging low over the water. The archer fish looks for a still target, seldom aiming at insects that are moving. In like fashion Satan aims his darts at the idle Christian. The best insurance against such attacks is to keep active. Those who keep busy for God are least likely to fall prey to the enemy.

Walter Cronkite, noted CBS commentator, declared: "I can't imagine a person becoming a success who doesn't give this game of life everything he's got."

In an earlier year, Theodore Roosevelt said the same thing another way: "When you play, play with all your might, but when you work, don't play at all. No man can hope to be outstandingly successful at anything unless he exerts the effort to run an extra undemanded mile."

Paul J. Meyer suggests several ways whereby an employer may make his employees work as hard as he does: 1) Encourage the employee to beat your system —earning incentive pay; 2) offer the employee security; 3) get the employee to set goals for himself; 4) set up hurdles to test for maximum potential; 5) permit the employee to work in his own style; 6) let the employee tell you how he needs to improve.

Meyer considers the establishment of good work habits one of the chief requisites to maximum production and efficiency. "A prime essential in developing good work habits," he says, "is having your own 'self-starter,' your own 'go' button. This isn't something that will come from the outside—it's a quality that must be developed from within. It takes personal motivation. Each of us marches to the drumbeat he hears within himself.

"Good work habits help develop an internal toughness and a self-confident attitude that will sustain you through every adversity and temporary discouragement. Good work habits make your work more enjoyable—and you more enthusiastic."

One of the strong adherents of good work habits is

G. Tom Willey, who was Vice-president and General Manager of Martin-Orlando before his recent retirement. "A coffee break," Willey once said, "is for competitors, or those who have nothing to do—and these people don't exist around here." Another time he observed that "nothing is done while you're discussing why it can't be done."

Hard work still pays rich dividends to the person who is conscientious. No genuine accomplishment in life ever comes without it. To the person who finds it physically impossible, or difficult, to be energetic, there may be a way out. An extra half an hour a day spent walking and jogging can work wonders for the tired, rundown body if it is done gradually and regularly. Begin slowly by walking, and stop before the body becomes obviously overtired. As the legs get into better shape, extend the walking and add a touch of jogging to the routine. Slowly but surely, the body will respond to the regular exercise and strength will come to every member. The person who "has no time" for such a program surely will find time for the inevitable doctor's appointment that may be hastened by his failure to undertake regular exercise. The current American obsession with jogging may seem only a temporary craze to many, but it has much merit. Energy is a necessity for the successful person, and this is one way to insure physical stamina and to remain industrious far beyond the average age.

How To Be Energetic

1. Determine to give your best to every job, large or small.
2. Establish good work habits for yourself.

3. Go the extra mile in any responsibility that is given you.
4. Exercise your body sufficiently to maintain physical fitness.
5. If you don't feel energetic, try to act energetically, anyway. If you still do not feel energetic, consult your physician.

How Is My Get-up-and-go?

Answer *yes* or *no*. Statements that are not applicable to your life on a specific day should not be counted in your score for that day. Eight or more *yes* answers: *superior;* six or seven, *excellent;* four or five, *good;* two or three, *fair;* one or none, *poor.*

1. My energy has not been dissipated to any appreciable degree in wasteful pursuits of this day.
2. In order to retain a proper degree of energy I have taken good care of my body in eating and drinking wisely.
3. I have been conscious of the need for proper exercise to help toward maximum energy.
4. My schedule of sleep is maintained so as to provide a maximum amount of energy for my body.
5. I have been careful not to overdo in physical exertion that would stifle my energy.
6. Regardless of my like or dislike of certain duties, I performed them with consistent energy.
7. Even though my physical energy could have been improved, I made up for the lack with maximum spiritual and mental energy.
8. My daily habits are such as to provide maximum physical energy throughout the day.

9. I try to remind myself often that my body is the temple of the Holy Spirit and therefore deserves the best possible care.

10. Like the Psalmist, who said, "I will go in the strength of the Lord God . . ." (71:16), I realized today where my strength lay.

SUCCESS DIARY

Week No. 9   Dates......................**19**......**to**......................**19**......

Major Goal: Be Energetic!
Minor Goal: Be Resilient!

(Check appropriate scores for each day)

Achievement of Goals		Superior	Excellent	Good	Fair	Poor
Sunday	(Major)					
	(Minor)					
Monday	(Major)					
	(Minor)					
Tuesday	(Major)					
	(Minor)					
Wednesday	(Major)					
	(Minor)					
Thursday	(Major)					
	(Minor)					
Friday	(Major)					
	(Minor)					
Saturday	(Major)					
	(Minor)					

Remarks:

10.

Am I Scared of Myself in the Dark?

TAKE COURAGE: There are 365 "Fear nots" in the Bible
—one for every day in the year! "Courage is a special
kind of knowledge," David Ben-Gurion observed, "the
knowledge of how to fear what ought to be feared and
how not to fear what ought not to be feared."

Andrew Jackson said it differently: "One man with
courage makes a majority." A slightly different twist
came from Thomas Carlyle: "The courage we desire
and prize is not the courage to die decently but to live
manfully."

In the athletic realm, Paul "Bear" Bryant, coach of
the famed Alabama Crimson Tide football team, is
considered a hard-nosed practitioner of the art of discipline. But it must have taken raw courage to make
some of the decisions he has had to make under difficult circumstances. Near the end of the 1963 season,
with two major games to go, star quarterback Joe
Namath broke training. Despite urgent pleas from all
sides Bryant suspended his outstanding player. After
all, the athlete had failed to observe explicit rules. But
before Namath left the University of Alabama and
signed a reported $400,000 professional contract with
the New York Jets, he told Coach Bryant, "I want to
look you right in the eye and tell you that you were

right, and I want to thank you." The courage of one's convictions always pays dividends.

Some years ago an ocean liner was wrecked on a dangerous reef off the New England coast. As a coast guard boat set out to the rescue, the seasoned old captain was approached by an inexperienced crewman. "Sir," said the youthful, white-faced sailor, "the wind is offshore and the tide is running out. We can go out, but we can never come back."

"Launch the boat," replied the captain. "We have to go out. We don't have to come back!" That kind of courage, though rare, is not limited to any particular part of the world. Often it manifests itself most clearly under persecution.

During the Korean conflict, Japanese policemen told parishioners of a little country church in Korea that they could have no worship services at all—only Japanese Shinto shrine worship was allowed. A few weeks later one of the Japanese policemen told the pastor he could hold a service. Word spread far and wide and, when Sunday morning came, men, women, young people and children overflowed the church; many had walked up to ten miles to attend. As they began to sing the wonderful hymn they loved so much, "Nearer, My God, to Thee," the Japanese police locked the door from the outside, poured gallons of kerosene on the building and set it afire. When some parishioners tried to escape through the windows, a squad of Japanese policemen shot them. "Let's keep singing," the pastor said. And he continued the familiar words, "Alas! and did my Saviour bleed, and did my Sovereign die, would He devote that sacred head for such a worm as I." As the little roof came down upon them they sang: "But drops of grief can ne'er repay the debt of love I owe; Here, Lord, I give myself away, 'tis all that I can do." Many American soldiers, who saw the site of this amazing demonstration of Christian courage, have had their lives greatly influenced for good.

Courage comes in many different styles and disguises. As June Callwood reflected in her book, *Love, Hate, Fear, Anger and the Other Lively Emotions* (Doubleday and Company), "Courage is a private thing . . . a man who apologizes to his own son may have waded through crocodiles. . . . Courage in its highest form, moral courage, is what makes a man indestructible. And there is a momentum to it. Each act of courage adds to man's faith in himself, in the purpose and dignity of all life. By each brave act he enlarges his ability to be brave—and eventually the process is irreversible."

Of this characteristic Sir Winston Churchill said: "Courage is the first of human qualities because it is the quality which guarantees all others." Lack of this trait led Sidney Smith to observe: "A great deal of talent is lost to the world for want of a little courage. Every day sends to their graves obscure men whom timidity prevented from making a first effort."

And Paul J. Meyer observed: "Critics of salesmanship claim that somewhere between the American troops at Bunker Hill and today's suburbanites . . . somewhere between Andrew Carnegie's 'hard work' formula and the prevalent concern for 'fringe benefits' . . . modern salesmen have lost something. They call it intestinal fortitude; I call it guts, and I don't think it's lost or even misplaced."

In discussing another facet of the subject Meyer said: "There is more to be feared in not making mistakes than in making them. Does this sound paradoxical? It's not. The manager who fears making mistakes too much to risk making them, obviously won't make any. But neither will he learn or grow. He will stand still, or slide backwards, while others about him, with the courage to face up to the inevitable risk that is inherent in initiative, will thrust forward. In short, the status of the individual who plays it too safe will be in greater jeopardy than his more venturesome counterpart."

Attitude plays a significant part in courage. A young soldier, regaining consciousness after an operation, was told he had lost a leg. "I didn't lose it," he replied, "I gave it." In a similar vein, a young physician, leaving for service in China, faced a pungent question. "What can you do against war, famine and flood?" he was asked. "When it is dark about me," he replied, "I do not curse the darkness, I just light my candle."

Napoleon often referred to Marshal Michel Ney as the bravest man he had ever known. Yet, one morning before battle, Ney's knees trembled so badly he had trouble mounting his horse. When he finally reached the saddle, he shouted contemptuously, "Shake away, knees! You would shake worse than that if you knew where I am going to take you."

English novelist Arnold Bennett observed: "No one can possibly be satisfied, or happy, who feels that in some paramount affair he has failed to take up the challenge of life. For a voice within him, which none else can hear but which he cannot choke, will constantly be murmuring, 'You lacked courage. You ran away.' It is happier to be unhappy in the ordinary sense than to have to listen to the end of one's life to that dreadful interior verdict.''

Even Confucius had his view of the subject: ''To see what is right, and not to do·it, is want of courage.''

Victor Hugo had his own ideas of this quality. ''Have courage for the great sorrows of life, and patience for the small ones,'' he advised, ''and when you have laboriously accomplished your daily task, go to sleep in peace. God is awake.''

Henry Van Dyke defined courage in this way: ''It is the standing army of the soul which keeps it from conquest, pillage and slavery.''

Another good definition appeared in an issue of *Goodall News,* published by the Goodall Rubber Co.: ''Courage is not a reckless indifference to death and danger but a striving towards a worthwhile goal which brave men, and often cowards, seek to attain even at the sacrifice of personal comfort, pleasure and immediate self-interest.''

Courage comes from the resurgence of hope after crushing disappointments, a man once observed. ''It comes from failure and the mastering of failure,'' he continued. ''It comes from discouragement and the overcoming of discouragement. No one can develop great courage until he has won victories over defeat. And no man knows if he possesses courage until he has faced failure.''

IBM executive T. J. Watson, Jr., said that ''every time we have moved ahead in IBM it was because someone was willing to take a chance, put his head on the block, and try something new.''

1. Act with courage, even when you do not feel courageous.
2. Look for the brighter side of every situation.
3. Stick by your convictions regardless of cost.
4. Remember, "God has not given you the spirit of fear"—and since fear comes from the enemy of men's souls, refuse to accept it.

Am I Scared of Myself in the Dark?

Answer *yes* or *no*. Statements that are not applicable to your life on a specific day should not be counted in your score for that day. Eight or more *yes* answers: *superior;* six or seven, *excellent;* four or five, *good;* two or three, *fair;* one or none, *poor.*

1. I found opportunity today to distinguish between foolhardiness and courage.
2. Although I knew a certain course of action would not be popular with other members of my family (company, class) I moved ahead, with the conviction that it was the right move.
3. I faced certain criticism for a right stand on an important matter of principle, but I did not flinch at sticking to that stand.
4. When a neighbor (or classmate, or associate) ridiculed a view which I believed right I did not retract that view.
5. I made a positive and determined step toward reducing one of my fears.
6. At the appropriate time, I found it possible to remain silent when I was unable to say something

kind or favorable about the person under discussion.

7. I was able, and willing, to speak up to correct false statements or impressions that were given about someone else.

8. Today I had the courage to fear those things which should be feared: cowardice, apathy, sin, et cetera.

9. In a difficult situation I was able to count upon the boldness that comes from confidence in God.

10. Recognizing that "God has not given us the spirit of fear, but of power, and of love, and of a sound mind," I refused to accept such fear today.

SUCCESS DIARY

Week No. 10   Dates.....................19...... to ....19......

Major Goal: Be Courageous!
Minor Goal: Be Energetic!

(Check appropriate scores for each day)

Achievement of Goals		Superior	Excellent	Good	Fair	Poor
Sunday	(Major)					
	(Minor)					
Monday	(Major)					
	(Minor)					
Tuesday	(Major)					
	(Minor)					
Wednesday	(Major)					
	(Minor)					
Thursday	(Major)					
	(Minor)					
Friday	(Major)					
	(Minor)					
Saturday	(Major)					
	(Minor)					

Remarks:

11.
Faith: Is Mine the Size of a Mustard Seed?

FAITH COMES in several different styles, sizes and packages. The ordinary garden variety is so taken for granted that it is rarely defined or recognized. But genuine faith is worthy of cultivation for the person who would be a success. It is more than normal confidence that the chair in which you sit will hold you up or that the pilot and crew of the plane on which you fly will see you through to a safe landing. It is the "substance of things hoped for, the evidence of things not seen" (Hebrews 11:1). But why is this brand of faith so essential to the successful man? And how is it expressed in practical ways?

Staunch old Admiral Farragut of the American Navy, he of the true heart and iron will, said to a fellow officer of the Navy, "Du Pont, do you know why you didn't get into Charleston with your ironclads?" "Oh, it was because the channel was so crooked." "No, Du Pont, it wasn't that." "Well, the rebel fire was perfectly horrible." "Yes, but it wasn't that." "What was it, then?" "It was because you didn't believe you could get in."

Belief is not everything, but it is a lot. As someone

once observed, "If there should arise one utterly believing man, the history of the world might be changed." Goethe expressed himself on the subject years ago: "If you have any certainties let us have them. We have doubts enough of our own."

Two friends of David Enlow—George Jobe and Neil Reynhout, Chicago area businessmen—accompanied him on a mission of mercy one evening. A parolee from an Eastern prison, witnessed to earlier concerning his spiritual welfare, had asked for a return visit to his apartment on Chicago's near South Side, so he could ask further questions. After they arrived at the apartment, the three men invited the former prisoner to a nearby restaurant for coffee and pie as they talked. Driving back, Enlow listened intently to the conversation behind him—so intently, in fact, that he overlooked a signal light that had been red for a few seconds.

Less than half a block later, a flashing light indicated the inevitable approach of the law. Asked to show his driver's license, Enlow pulled out his wallet and flashed the card. To his dismay, the officer's glance revealed that something was amiss: the license had expired several days earlier. The red-faced driver was guilty on two counts. But he felt particularly bad about the fact that his friend Jobe had counted on completing the mission in sufficient time to report for his night job. A trip to the station would make that impossible.

The officer seemed completely unsympathetic to the problem, explaining that he could not overlook two such violations. He asked Enlow to follow him to the station. The dejected driver retreated toward his car, but he had moved only a few steps before the officer called him back. "Here you are," he said, holding out the license, "but don't let it happen again. Get that license renewed right away."

Jubilant at the outcome, Enlow returned to his car expecting surprise and unbelief from his three companions. Reynhout looked at him calmly after he heard the story. "We'd be surprised if anything else had happened," he said. "The moment you left the car we reminded the Lord we were on His business; He knew about the problem; and we were going to trust Him to work it out!"

All of the men learned an unforgettable lesson. Faith can be so real that it is like cashing a check on the Bank of Heaven. These men had done that very thing and it had been honored. Of course, the most important factor was the source of their faith. They had not believed in the officer, or in Enlow's ability to talk himself out of it—they had believed in God. Because it was well-founded, their faith became substance.

Many things go into the matter of believing. William Jennings Bryan, statesman of yesteryear, marveled at one particular aspect of faith: "I was eating a piece of watermelon some months ago and was struck with its beauty. I took some of the seeds and weighed them and found that it would require some five thousand seeds to weigh a pound. And then I applied mathematics to a forty-pound melon. One of these seeds, put into the ground, when warmed by the sun and moistened by the rain goes to work; it gathers from somewhere two hundred thousand times its own weight and, forcing this raw material through a tiny stem, constructs a watermelon."

Bryan continued: "It covers the outside with a coating of green; inside of the green it puts a layer of white, and within the white a core of red, and all through the red it scatters seeds, each one capable of continuing the work of reproduction. I cannot explain the watermelon, but I eat it and enjoy it. Everything that grows tells a like story of infinite power. Why should I deny that a divine hand fed a multitude with a few loaves and fishes when I see hundreds of millions fed every year by a hand which converts the seeds scattered over the field into an abundant harvest? We know that food can be multiplied in a few months' time. Shall we deny the power of the Creator to eliminate the element of time, when we have gone so far in eliminating the element of space?"

A significant observation on believing comes from James F. Oates, Jr., Chairman of the Board of The Equitable Life Assurance Society of the U. S. "If a person genuinely looks for faith," he said, "he will find it. A person should seek it, I think, from those who have it, not from cynical disbelievers. One never finds the answer for belief in men or books or vocations committed to disbelief." In the final analysis, of course, "faith comes by hearing, and hearing by the Word of God."

David Lawrence, Publisher of *U. S. News and World Report,* declared that "the destiny of the world is in the hands of those statesmen who can faithfully interpret the commands of the Almighty."

Adding to the subject of faith, Charles L. Allen, minister of the First Methodist Church in Houston, Texas, lists three guiding principles toward happiness: 1) Be yourself; 2) make up your mind; 3) learn to believe. "If any person expects to succeed," Dr. Allen says, "he must first learn to believe. I say learn to believe because it must be learned. We had to learn how to walk. Before we learned, we probably fell many times, but we can walk now because we kept on trying after each fall.

"At the very center of the Christian faith is an eternal, all-powerful God. When one starts with God, putting his belief first in Him, it makes the major difference. You cannot do it by yourself, but with His help you can eventually really know what St. Paul meant when he said, 'I can do all things through Christ which strengtheneth me.'"

Another man of the cloth, the late Bishop William A. Quayle, used to tell of an experience he had during a sleepless night. After rolling and tossing far into the night, he seemed to hear God's voice telling him to go on to sleep and to let God run the world for the rest of the night.

"Seeing is believing," according to an old familiar adage. Yet things are not always what they seem. An unknown author of the fourteenth century made this observation: "I judge that jeweler unworthy of praise who wholly believes what he sees with his eye." Man's power of perception is vastly limited, in spite of the tremendous area which science has brought into focus. All of his senses are not now as perfect or complete as God will one day make them, and he must take this into account when he determines what he knows and believes.

For instance, when one stands between the two rails of a railroad track and looks into the distance, the parallel rails seem to converge into a single rail. Yet this is not so. When the world seems completely silent, a dog may lift his ears, indicating that he has heard a sound of which his master is unaware. A block of steel, according to the sense of touch, is solid. But the physicist, having studied and tested solids, knows that all solids are composed of innumerable little universes, each independent of and separated from the next, and all are in rapid motion.

So, before believing, we must examine that evidence which is beyond what we know by our senses. Then, determining that the evidence warrants our acceptance, we believe. This is faith, that "substance" to which we referred earlier.

An internationally famous surgeon, Howard A. Kelly, M.D., F.A.C.S., Johns Hopkins University, in describing his emergence into faith, declared: "I put my Bible to the practical test of noting what it says about itself, and then tested it to see how it worked. I looked up 'Word' in the concordance and noted that the Bible claims from Genesis 1 to Revelation 22 to be God's personal message to man.

"The next traditional step then was to accept it as the authoritative textbook of the Christian faith just as one would accept a treatise on any earthly 'science,' and I submitted to its conditions according to Christ's invitation and promise that 'If any man will do his will, he shall know of the doctrine, whether it be of God, or whether I speak of myself' (John 7:17). The outcome of such an experiment has been in due time the acceptance of the Bible as the Word of God inspired in a sense utterly different from any merely human book, and with it the acceptance of our Lord Jesus Christ as the only begotten Son of God, Son of Man by the Virgin Mary, the Saviour of the world."

Another man who thought his way through to a reasoning faith was John Wesley. "I beg leave," he once said, "to give a short, clear, strong argument for the divine inspiration of the Holy Scriptures. The Bible must be the invention of good men or angels, bad men or devils, or of God. It could not be the invention of good men or angels, for they neither would or could make a book and tell lies all the time they are writing it, saying 'Thus saith the Lord,' when it was their own invention.''

Wesley continued: "It could not be the invention of bad men or devils, for they could not make a book which commands all duty, forbids all sins, and condemns their own souls to hell for all eternity. Therefore I draw the conclusion that the Bible must be given by divine inspiration.'' The corollary is that if it is God's Word and true we can believe all it says.

Missionary Fred Jarvis told the authors: "If a man is going to be successful, he must cut out the word 'impossible' from his dictionary. Faith translates desire into reality or its physical counterpart. Faith is the eternal elixir. It is the only antidote to failure. Faith is the starting point of all success, the basis of all miracles. If you think you are beaten, you are. The man who wins is the man who thinks he can. Faith demands and expects God to answer. Faith is creative; it makes things happen. Beethoven was deaf; Milton was blind; Helen Keller was both deaf and blind. It takes the fuel of fasting or the furnace of affliction to generate the fires of faith. Fear is faith in the wrong object. Fear God, but nothing else. Faith cures and casts out fear. Exercise your faith; don't fertilize your fears. We can believe and receive, or doubt and do without.''

What really is faith? As previously stated, it is "the substance of things hoped for, the evidence of things not seen.'' It comes by "hearing, and hearing by the Word of God.'' In short, genuine faith is a gift from

God. It cannot be bought or merited. But it can be obtained by obedience to His Word. No successful person ever reached that happy state without first believing that he would. In like fashion, we can harness our faith to do great exploits and to attain high goals. It is up to us.

How To Be Believing

1. Be sure the basis of your faith is worthy of your belief and trust.
2. Learn from believers, not from unbelievers.
3. Make the Word of God your textbook.
4. Cultivate the art of believing the good and the best, knowing that "all things work together for good to them that love God."

Faith: Is Mine the Size of a Mustard Seed?

Answer *yes* or *no*. Statements that are not applicable to your life on a specific day should not be counted in your score for that day. Eight or more *yes* answers: *superior;* six or seven, *excellent;* four or five, *good;* two or three, *fair;* one or none, *poor*.

1. My attitude in the home (at the office, at school) was one of a positive, believing nature in the inherent good will of others.
2. Crude actions or statements of others failed to mar or hinder my belief.
3. Other evidence to the contrary, I chose to believe only the best about anyone with whom I had any dealings today.
4. A firm belief in the sure knowledge that One still

sits on the throne of the universe eased my way this day.

5. By faith I considered all things today to have worked together for my good.

6. Despite adverse conditions I have pressed on this day to a more sure belief in the ruling and reigning power of God in my life.

7. I believed certain things this day almost solely by faith—having confidence in the promises of God—which gave me courage to stand by my convictions and brought me closer to attaining my goal.

8. My believing today was mostly centered around the Person of the Lord Jesus Christ.

9. My faith this day was recognized in itself to be a gift of God.

10. By a deliberate act of the will I chose to believe God today even if it meant to adjudge "every man a liar."

SUCCESS DIARY

Week No. 11   Dates...................19...... to ....19......

Major Goal: Be Believing!
Minor Goal: Be Courageous!

(Check appropriate scores for each day)

Achievement of Goals		Superior	Excellent	Good	Fair	Poor
Sunday	(Major)					
	(Minor)					
Monday	(Major)					
	(Minor)					
Tuesday	(Major)					
	(Minor)					
Wednesday	(Major)					
	(Minor)					
Thursday	(Major)					
	(Minor)					
Friday	(Major)					
	(Minor)					
Saturday	(Major)					
	(Minor)					

Remarks:

12.
Why Pray When I Can Worry?

ADDRESSING the Constitutional Convention, Benjamin
Franklin declared: "When we were in great peril we
had daily prayers in this room for the protection and
guidance of Almighty God. I have lived a long time,
and the longer I live the more convincing proof I have
that God governs in the affairs of men. If a sparrow
cannot fall to the earth without His knowledge, is it
possible for a nation to rise without His aid? To that
kind Providence we owe this happy privilege of con-
sulting in peace on the means of establishing our future national felicity. Have we now forgotten that
powerful friend; or have we no longer need of His as-
sistance?"

Not only the famous, but also the virtually unknown,
have found victory—personally and collectively—in
the unfathomable power of prayer. One night during
the Revolutionary War a British soldier was caught
creeping stealthily back to his quarters from the
nearby woods. He was taken before his commanding
officer and charged with communicating with the enemy. The man pleaded that he had gone into the woods
to pray. That was his only defense.

"Have you been in the habit of spending hours in
private prayer?" the officer growled.

"Yes, sir."

"Then down on your knees and pray now! You never needed it so much!"

Expecting immediate death, the soldier knelt and poured out his heart in a prayer so eloquent it could have been inspired only by the power of the Holy Spirit.

"You may go," said the officer simply, when the soldier had finished. "I believe your story. If you hadn't drilled often, you couldn't have done so well at review."

The value of intercession is evidenced in the military field, and in the realm of business also. James L. Kraft, founder of Kraft Foods Company, when asked the recipe for his success, which went into building the largest enterprise of its kind in the world from an original capital investment of only sixty-five dollars, replied:

"The safest, surest and swiftest road to victory is prayer, the habit of prayer which was once the familiar, everyday blessing it was intended to be in this nation. Its blessings are as powerful today as ever, if we would utilize them. Personal and family prayer, practiced daily in quietness of spirit, could, I believe, alter the whole world, as I know it alters individual lives."

Such a view of prayer belongs not alone to the successful businessman or the military figure. Expressing his feelings in picturesque language, Alfred Lord Tennyson wrote:

More things are wrought by prayer
Than this world dreams of.

Wherefore, let thy voice
Rise like a fountain for me night and day.
For what are men better than sheep or goats
That nourish a blind life within the brain,
If, knowing God, they lift not hands of prayer
Both for themselves and those who call them friends?
For so the whole round earth is every way
Bound by bold chains about the feet of God.

—*Morte d'Arthur*

How can you apply this habit of prayer personally to your own life? Set aside definite times for communion with God; remain in a spirit of prayer throughout the day, bathing every plan and every decision in prayer, seeking divine guidance and direction and wisdom from God constantly. After all, He, and He alone, knows exactly what we should do and just how we should do it in order to attain the goals He has set before us.

This does not mean simply asking God to bless our plans and to bring them to fruition. It means seeking, with a receptive and open mind and heart, His plan and His purpose and His method. After determining these through Scripture and direct guidance, every detail should be committed to God, then bathed in prayer.

God knows the perfect plan for our lives, as well as every detail of its attainment. We do not know. The realization of this simple and obvious fact should make us both humble and prayerful. We should pray about everything. Nothing is too small or too great to pray about. Once we belong to God, through faith in His Son Jesus Christ, He is interested in the minutest detail of our lives because of His love for us. Because He is omnipotent He knows every detail and He is able to answer every prayer and solve every problem. There is no degree of difficulty with God.

In his insurance business Arthur DeMoss has received great satisfaction and help by saturating every decision with prayer—every position to be filled, every problem or even potential problem—constantly seeking wisdom from God, asking that His perfect will be done. How wonderful to see God answer prayer! How thrilling to see Him work out apparently hopeless problems in the most remarkable ways; to see Him bring the seemingly impossible to pass time and again!

The joy of seeing one's own plans flounder, and then watching God do something far greater and more wonderful can be attributed to prayer and the power of prayer. Basic to success in this particular area of life is our concept of prayer. Prayer is not some mystical mumbo-jumbo. Nor is it a question of mind over matter, or autosuggestion, or anything of this sort. Rather it is like a child coming to his Father and seeking—confident that his Father loves him enough to want to do for him what is best, that He *knows* what is best and has the ability to grant it.

But, unless and until He is our Father, we have no right to go to Him in prayer—except as a sinner in search of a Saviour. The Scriptures make it clear that while He is Creator He is not the Father of everyone, but only of those who have been born again into His family by faith in His Son Jesus Christ. There can be no real success without knowing God and belonging to Him. The apparent success which some people seem to enjoy not only turns to dust and ashes, but also it cannot *really* be enjoyed because without Christ there can be no lasting peace or joy or happiness.

In the field of politics, many Congressmen believe in

the power of prayer and act clearly upon that belief, as evidenced by the Senate and House prayer groups that meet regularly. Senator Frank Carlson of Kansas told the authors: "I am a firm believer in the efficacy of prayer, the power of Christ to save, and a very personal, everyday religion. The words of St. James, 'The effectual, fervent prayer of a righteous man availeth much,' have been a help and consolation to me on many occasions. In this period of unrest, uncertainty and distress I would recommend to our individual citizens and this nation as a whole that we get back to the principles advocated by the Man who walked the shores of Galilee two thousand years ago."

Representative Chester L. Mize, also of Kansas, declared: "One of the most meaningful and continuing experiences I enjoy as a member of Congress is my attendance at the Thursday morning prayer breakfast, held by and for members of the House of Representatives. Different members of the House conduct the weekly programs, discussing personal religious experiences or a subject relative to Christianity. All attending, both Democrats and Republicans, are dedicated Christians, gentlemen of the highest moral caliber. It is most refreshing to spend this one hour a week in this magnificent atmosphere."

Many of our men in the military services likewise turn to prayer as the only help. In a letter to his sister, a Lieutenant in the United States Army sounded as clear a call to prayer as this nation will ever hear: "Prayer is going to win this war. Not guns alone. Fervent, agonizing prayer. Pray, Sis. Pray as you never prayed before. Tell everyone to pray. Tell all America to get to its knees. Before each decisive victory anywhere over here, sometimes for hours, sometimes for days, there has been a feeling of people praying from far away. The feeling is so strong that you can hear it. One of the most stubborn of the men said, in the stillness of the night, 'Did you hear anything? Sounded like people praying from some distant place.' ''

Getting back to the realm of business: Robert P. Woodburn, Vice-president of the National Bank of Washington, D. C., known far and wide for his effective, man-to-man, personal witness, revealed to the authors his open secret: "Always make sure the Lord has priority each day, from the standpoint of beginning the morning with God's Word and prayer, then by walking and talking with Him throughout the day." Mr. Woodburn attributes the phenomenal success of his bank operation to prayer which prompted this comment from a former president of the bank: "In prayer you are not on a party line like the rest; you seem to have a direct line to God."

The chief cartoonist of *Chicago's American,* Vaughn Shoemaker, winner of two Pulitzer Prizes in May of 1950, insists that any degree of success he has achieved came through prayer. His philosophy of prayer is evident in his assertion that "if we think we are able to run our lives, God will step aside and let us do our best. But if we will admit we haven't anything of ourselves and turn to Him, He will work miracles every day. God creates a miracle when there is no other person we can give the credit to."

Sometimes a miracle seems to be the only way out of a dilemma, and it is at such times that God loves to show Himself. A missionary wife in Africa suddenly became ill. Although her husband did everything he could for her, she steadily grew worse. On the third day it seemed she surely would die. Almost delirious, she whispered to her husband that she believed she would get well if she could have some tomatoes. That only added to her husband's anguish, for where in such a wilderness would he find such a delicacy? He began to pray.

The following morning a native woman appeared at the door, a basket on her arm. She had a simple request. A white man had left her tribe some seeds several months earlier; she had planted them and now she wanted to know if the result was edible. Lifting the cover on the basket, the missionary was astounded to see three ripe tomatoes. He bought those tomatoes, bought more, and fed them to his wife. She recovered from her illness, as though in rebuke to her husband's lack of faith. The same God who had fed the five thousand had no problem in supplying the needed tomatoes.

In the Midwest a top executive experienced the dynamic power of prayer in his life. Herbert J. Taylor, former Chairman of the Board of the Club Aluminum Products Company, LaGrange, Illinois, and past president of Rotary International, started with that company way back in 1932, when he was assigned by the creditors of the firm the task of saving the company from going bankrupt.

"We felt that we must develop within our organization something which our competitors would not have in equal amount," Taylor said. "We decided that it should be the character, dependability and service-mindedness of our personnel. When I don't have the answer to a problem I turn to my Heavenly Father. So one day I asked God to give me a simple measuring stick of ethics for our company. Shortly thereafter I took out a card and wrote out the *Four-Way Test:* 1) Is it the truth? 2) Is it fair to all concerned? 3) Will it build good-will and better friendships? 4) Will it benefit all concerned?"

That simple test has been widely acclaimed and used throughout the world as a principle of business ethics.

Referring to this critical era in world history, Taylor says: "Oh, how we need to pray! How we need to turn away from material, worldly things and humbly bow down in prayer to the source of all power, all love, all wisdom. Let us all take time to pray daily for God's guidance, for His will for each one of us, for His all-powerful intervention in our behalf."

In a similar vein, the late Roger Babson once declared: "The greatest undeveloped resource of our country is faith. The greatest unused power is prayer. People must get back to God. For a long time it has been considered rather smart to be irreligious. Now people must get back to God. Above all, they should start praying. They seem to think there is something about prayer that is not exactly red-blooded or two-fisted. When business worries me, I think of God. If someone has been unkind to me, I think of God. If I should come face to face with disaster, I should think of God."

In earlier days, an officer once complained to General Stonewall Jackson that some soldiers were making a noise in their tent. "What are they doing?" asked the General. "They are praying now, but they have been singing," was the reply. "And is that a crime?" the General demanded. "The Articles of War order punishment for any unusual noise," came the reply. "God forbid that praying should be an unusual noise in this camp," replied General Jackson.

Once asked his understanding of the Bible command

to "pray without ceasing," the great Stonewall said, "I have so fixed the habit in my mind that I never raise a glass of water to my lips without lifting my heart to God in thanks and prayer for the water of life. Then, when we take our meals there is grace. Whenever I drop a letter in the post office I send a petition along with it for God's blessing upon its mission and the person to whom it is sent. When I go to my classroom and await the arrangement of the cadets in their places, that is my time to intercede with God for them. And so in every act of the day I have made the practice habitual."

Another who felt that way was the old Lancashire woman who was listening to the reasons neighbors gave for their minister's success. She heard them speak of his gifts, of his style, of his manner. "Nay," she said, "I tell you what it is. Yon man is very thick with the Almighty." The point is well made by people of all nations, races, creeds, colors; past, present and future: Christians need to return to prayer as their number one source of power.

Prayer has been called the breath of the Christian. As the intake of air keeps us alive physically, so the recourse to prayer helps to maintain our spiritual lives. It is an attitude that should be cultivated, but it is more than that. Prayer is the Christian's lifeline to the Almighty. May we not allow anything to break that vital contact with Deity.

How To Be Prayerful

1. Pray!
2. Read a Psalm to acquire and strengthen a spirit of prayer.

3. Practice the presence of Christ.
4. Set aside a specific time and place for daily prayer, ideally at the start of each day.
5. Make a habit of listening for the still, small voice of God an integral part of your prayer time.
6. Spend time in prayer even when you don't feel like praying.
7. Try praying aloud. The sound of your voice may distract you at first, but soon you will find yourself speaking more intelligently than ever and with power.
8. Like Moses, let God talk face to face with you, as a man speaks to his friend (Exodus 33:11).

WHY PRAY WHEN I CAN WORRY?

Answer *yes* or *no*. Statements that are not applicable to your life on a specific day should not be counted in your score for that day. Eight or more *yes* answers: *superior;* six or seven, *excellent;* four or five, *good;* two or three, *fair;* one or none, *poor.*

1. My first thought upon arising this morning was to spend time with the Lord.
2. At one or more times of decision today I breathed a silent prayer to God.
3. My prayer time usually is begun with this Scriptural injunction or its equivalent: "Open thou mine eyes that I may behold wondrous things out of thy law" (Psalm 119:18).
4. At times of prayer I have been conscious of the warning, "If I regard iniquity in my heart, the Lord will not hear me" (Psalm 66:18).
5. I have been aware of the fact that praise is a primary consideration in effective prayer.

6. When problems come to mind during periods of prayer, I am learning to commit them to the Lord.

7. Even when I do not feel like praying, the Scriptural command to "pray without ceasing" keeps me faithful to the task.

8. I was able to approach prayer time with the positive assurance that "according to your faith be it unto you."

9. My confidence at prayer time was in the power of an Almighty heavenly Father rather than in any man or even in some preconceived notion as to how I thought God might act to solve my problems.

10. My approach to God was as a little child.

SUCCESS DIARY

Week No. 12   Dates......................19...... to ....19......

Major Goal: Be Prayerful!
Minor Goal: Be Believing!

(Check appropriate scores for each day)

Achievement of Goals		Superior	Excellent	Good	Fair	Poor
Sunday	(Major)					
	(Minor)					
Monday	(Major)					
	(Minor)					
Tuesday	(Major)					
	(Minor)					
Wednesday	(Major)					
	(Minor)					
Thursday	(Major)					
	(Minor)					
Friday	(Major)					
	(Minor)					
Saturday	(Major)					
	(Minor)					

Remarks:

How to Change Your World
in Twelve Seconds

IF YOU HAVE followed the schedule conscientiously for the past twelve weeks—testing and grading yourself daily on the various characteristics—by now you should be convinced that success comes to those who prepare for it. But perhaps you feel that something is still lacking in your life; it leaves such a huge gap that you may feel as if no progress at all has been made.

If this describes or approximates your situation it is possible you have missed out on the most important phase of your life—the spiritual. Ultimately, real success in the fullest sense is not possible without knowing God in a vital way and His perfect plan for one's life. All that is required to accomplish an amazing transformation in your life can take place in a matter of seconds. An act of will is involved. And you can accomplish it all alone, in the quiet of your own home or office.

Even for the reader who has made this eternal transaction there is room for deeper commitment—one that can bring a new dimension to every area of your life and which can take place in a matter of seconds. But, for the moment, let us consider the person who has never dared to test the terms of the gospel as revealed in the Word of God—the Bible.

When the first man who ever lived, Adam, was created by the Lord, a perfect relationship existed between the creature and his Creator. Left to his own devices Adam deliberately broke that fellowship by disobeying God and thus introducing sin into the world. One man, Adam—our earthly father—first brought sin into the human race. A just and merciful God, however, desirous of fellowship with His own creation, determined to enable man to restore that perfect relationship. Even as one man, Adam, introduced sin into the world, so the Lord decided to make it possible for man to resume his former state through the divine intervention of One Man: God sent His own Son, Jesus Christ, into the world in human form to live as a divine Man and to die a cruel death on Calvary's Cross that would atone for the sins of all men who would believe.

To restore that relationship with the Creator on a personal basis today, only one condition is required of man: he must humble himself to the extent of acknowledging his own sinful condition, repent, confess and receive Christ into his heart and life by faith as personal Lord and Saviour, a deliberate act of the will that can be consummated in seconds. Often, the very simplicity of the act causes people to neglect the so great salvation provided by the Creator. Your decision to believe and receive is not conversion, but the divine act of accepting that decision and transforming one's life quickly brings about what the Bible calls the new birth, also called regeneration.

One cannot describe exactly what takes place at the time of regeneration; he can only tell of the transformation that results as life takes on meaning for the first time. In the apt words of one convert, it is as if God reaches down inside one's heart and turns on a light. One's goals—his aim and purpose in life—center around matters of eternity and of glorifying God rather than revolving around mere material security and a sense of belonging. One's entire outlook becomes different. One still may do wrong—sin against God—but he is not happy in his sin and he has a remedy: "If we confess our sins, he is faithful and just to forgive us our sins, and to cleanse us from all unrighteousness" (I John 1:9).

The new Christian quickly discovers an appetite for 1) *prayer*—conversing with his Heavenly Father; 2) *reading the Word of God,* the Bible—God's love letter to His creatures; 3) *fellowship* with others who believe as he does and thereby are members of the same family—the wonderful, glorious Body of Christ. He soon realizes also that God has a plan for his life and that he may discover that plan by diligent searching: "If any of you lack wisdom, let him ask of God, that giveth to all men liberally, and upbraideth not; and it shall be given him" (James 1:5). His daily schedule is geared toward making his entire life a stewardship—of time, talent and money. Remarkable indeed is the fact that this salvation can take place in a matter of seconds—by an act of will that accepts and receives Jesus Christ as a result of His finished work on the Cross.

Second only to the remarkable transformation that accompanies salvation is that which is wrought by the Lord in the heart and life of one who has reached a place of full commitment so that he is ready for the empowering and enabling of God's Holy Spirit in his life in a greater way than he ever dreamed possible.

Like the initial act of regeneration such empowering can take place in a matter of seconds. Primarily the will is involved but, as with conversion, the emotions hardly can be bypassed completely in such a life-changing decision.

Alertness to the still, small voice of God's Holy Spirit characterizes the man or woman, young or old, who has made either or both of these major steps. That, along with the "love of God shed abroad in the heart," is the acid test of sincere commitment. And, in reality, no life can be considered a success without some touch with the eternal. "For what shall it profit a man, if he shall gain the whole world, and lose his own soul? Or what shall a man give in exchange for his soul?" (Mark 8:36-7).

Presumably, you are dead serious about making a success of your life or you would not have read thus far. Therefore, we want to speak quite frankly in this closing chapter. In the eyes of the world, your road to success can be smoothed immeasurably by cultivating the twelve qualities referred to in these pages: receptivity, enthusiasm, single-mindedness, perseverance, time-consciousness, flexibility, confidence, resilience, energy, courage, faith, prayerfulness. All of these characteristics will hasten your progress toward achievement of whatever worthwhile goals you have set for your life.

An added dimension—eternity—can become an integral part of that plan for your life and can make it all seem—and be—more worthwhile than ever. Success, one might say, is a many splendored thing, depending upon whose definition is considered. But the important thing for our purposes is your own interpretation of the word. What have you set out to accomplish in your "three-score-and-ten"? Do you see your way clearer toward achievement of these goals? If so, we feel that this book is a success and our time and efforts have been rewarded.